THE FATHERS
OF THE CHURCH

A NEW TRANSLATION

VOLUME 52

THE FATHERS
OF THE CHURCH

A NEW TRANSLATION

EDITORIAL BOARD

ROY JOSEPH DEFERRARI
The Catholic University of America
Editorial Director

MSGR. JAMES A. MAGNER
The Catholic University of America

BERNARD M. PEEBLES
The Catholic University of America

MARTIN R. P. MCGUIRE
The Catholic University of America

REV. THOMAS HALTON
The Catholic University of America

ROBERT P. RUSSELL, O.S.A.
Villanova University

WILLIAM R. TONGUE
The Catholic University of America

HERMIGILD DRESSLER, O.F.M.
The Catholic University of America

REV. PETER J. RAHILL
The Catholic University of America

SISTER M. JOSEPHINE BRENNAN, I.H.M.
Marywood College

THE POEMS
OF PRUDENTIUS

VOLUME 2

Translated by
SISTER M. CLEMENT EAGAN, C.C.V.I.
Incarnate Word College
San Antonio, Texas

THE CATHOLIC UNIVERSITY OF AMERICA PRESS, Inc.
Washington, D. C. 20017

NIHIL OBSTAT:
REVEREND HARRY A. ECHLE
Censor Librorum

IMPRIMATUR:
✠ PATRICK A. O'BOYLE
Archbishop of Washington

January 11, 1965

The *nihil obstat* and *imprimatur* are official declarations that a book or pamphlet is free of doctrinal or moral error. No implication is contained therein that those who have granted the *nihil obstat* and *imprimatur* agree with the contents, opinions, or statements expressed.

Library of Congress Catalog Card No. 63-5499

Copyright © 1965 by
THE CATHOLIC UNIVERSITY OF AMERICA PRESS, INC.
All rights reserved

First Paperback Reprint 2011
ISBN 978-0-8132-1872-4

THE POEMS
OF PRUDENTIUS

VOLUME 2

APOLOGETIC AND DIDACTIC POEMS

CONTENTS

	Page
INTRODUCTION	ix
THE DIVINITY OF CHRIST	3
THE ORIGIN OF SIN	43
THE SPIRITUAL COMBAT	79
AGAINST SYMMACHUS, BOOK ONE	113
AGAINST SYMMACHUS, BOOK TWO	139
SCENES FROM SACRED HISTORY, or TWOFOLD NOURISHMENT	179
EPILOGUE	199
INDICES	203

INTRODUCTION

THIS IS THE SECOND of the two volumes into which the present translation of the poems of Prudentius has been divided, as was indicated in the Introduction to Volume 1. The previous volume, Volume 43 of this Series, contained the two books of hymns: the *Liber Cathemerinon,* 'Book of Hymns for Every Day,' and the *Liber Peristephanon,* 'Book of the Martyrs' Crowns.' These lyric poems are written in a variety of Latin classical meters.

The present volume contains the didactic and apologetic works of Prudentius, the *Apotheosis, Hamartigenia, Psychomachia,* and *Contra Symmachum,* all long poems written in dactylic hexameters and preceded by lyrical prefaces; the *Tituli historiarum* or *Dittochaeon* consisting of forty-nine hexameter quatrains; and the *Epilogue.*

In the *Apotheosis,* a poem of 1084 hexameters, Prudentius refutes the early heretics of the Church who denied the orthodox doctrine of the Trinity and the divinity of Christ. The *Hamartigenia,* or 'Origin of Sin,' is a refutation of the heretic Marcion who taught that there were two Gods, one the author of evil and the other the author of good. The *Psychomachia* is a long allegorical epic, in which Virtues and Vices contend for mastery in the human soul. In the first book of the *Contra Symmachum,* Prudentius attacks the pagan gods of Rome; in the second, he refutes the arguments of Symmachus for the restoration of the statue of Victory in the Senate House and the recognition of the pagan religion. The first twenty-four quatrains of the *Tituli historiarum* or *Dittochaeon,* 'Scenes from Sacred History or Twofold Nourishment,' deal with episodes from the Old Testament, and the remaining twenty-five are descriptive of scenes from the New Testament. Commentators are of the opinion that these quatrains were intended to serve as inscriptions for pictures or mosaics in a church. The *Epilogue,* in which the poet humbly offers his works to God, concludes this second volume.

The long apologetic poems in this volume have been translated into blank verse, the best English medium for rendering the Latin dactylic hexameter. As in the translation of the hymns of the first volume, the lyrical prefaces have been rendered in the English accentual equivalents of the various classical meters. The text used is that of Bergman, Volume 61, of the *Corpus Scriptorum Ecclesiasticorum Latinorum.*

THE DIVINITY OF CHRIST

(APOTHEOSIS)

THE DIVINITY OF CHRIST

A Hymn on The Trinity

Trinity highest is God, three in person and one in His essence;
Wisdom born of the Father's heart is His Son and beloved,
And the Spirit all Holy proceeds from that fountain eternal.
Neither older in time is the Father, nor greater in Godhead,
For from Himself the eternal God all-knowing engendered   5
That Divine Word through whom all created things have
    their being.[1]
While to beget the Word is alone the work of the Father,
To the Word it belongs to save man by assuming his nature,
To make amends for him to the Father and bring him to
    heaven.
This is the role of the Spirit of God, who Himself is true
    Godhead: 10
Ever ready to pour out His gifts on the souls of the faithful,
He applies to their hearts the graces of Christ and the Father.

Preface

Is our religion true? Thee, Master, I consult.
    Do we unswerving faith maintain,
Or do we, heedless of the bane of teachings false,
    Lapse into error unawares?
Amid the winding paths salvation's narrow way[1]   5
    Can scarce be traced with certainty,

---
1 Cf. John 1.3.

---
1 Cf. Matt. 7.14.

So many crossroads loom before us, trodden smooth
   By wanderers straying from the faith,
And hidden bypaths are encountered on the way
   Where here and there the tracks entwine.   10
If wandering from the truth man follows these detours
   And leaves the straight and narrow road,
He soon will fall headlong into the hidden snare
   That enemies have set for him,
A robber band that falls upon the travelers,   15
   When they pursue a devious way.
What does the boldness of the human mind not frame?
   What evils does it not desire?
The nature of Almighty God men dare assail
   With false and quibbling arguments.   20
They cut the faith to pieces with the subtle cant
   That flows from their malicious tongues.
They settle and unravel every knotty point
   By labyrinthine sophistries.
Woe to these hypocrites and their deceitful wiles!   25
   Woe to their cunning trickery!
True faith, the foe to these misleading disputants,
   Asunder rends the hardest knot.
God has expressly chosen foolish things of earth
   To vanquish and confound the wise,[2]   30
And by the weak things He has overcome the strong
   To make it easy to believe.
Behold a stone is set for us, a stumbling block,[3]
   Against which vanity may strike,
A sign unto the faithful, scandal to the lax,   35
   The one it fells, the other guides.
The blind man feels his way with slow uncertain step
   And runs into what'er he meets.

---

[2] Cf. 1 Cor. 1.27.
[3] Cf. 1 Peter 2.7,8.

The lamp of faith alone must shine before our feet,[4]
   That footsteps may unswerving be.   40
The foe assails and carries off the wanderers
   Who in the darkness go astray,
A demon who devours the wheat spread on the way
   For pilgrims passing to and fro,
A thief who tampers with the fertile fields of Christ   45
   By sowing in them barren oats.[5]
The husbandman allows these, fed by poison sap,
   To grow into the ripened plant,
Lest he, perchance, by rooting up the useless tares
   Should kill the stalk that bears the grain.[6]   50
He waits, therefore, until the glowing harvest time
   When both the good and bad are ripe,
That what his fan has winnowed may be stored in barns,
   And chaff with fire may be consumed.[7]
Yet it behooves all men to understand the seed   55
   Of tares that choke the golden crop.

Of countless errors, few my song shall treat
Lest naming them, I stain my faithful tongue.
One banishing the Father from His throne,[1]
Clothes Him in narrow human frame,[2] nor fears
To make Him die, nailed to the bitter tree.[3]   5
Can Godhead suffer, God whose form and shape
Was never seen, for thought or eye or hand

---

[4] Cf. Ps. 118.105
[5] Cf. Matt. 13.25.
[6] Cf. Matt. 13.29,30.
[7] Cf. Matt. 3.12.

[1] Cf. Claudian, *De bello Gildonico* 409.
[2] Cf. Claudian, *In Rufinum* 2.487.
[3] The chief proponents of the Trinitarian heresy of the first centuries known as Monarchianism, Patripassianism, or Modalism were Noetus, Praxeas, and Sabellius. They held that there is no distinction of divine Persons in God, but only one Principle, the Father who created the world, became incarnate, and died for men. They considered the Trinity as three modes of being and self-manifestation of the one God, who is the Father insofar as He is the Creator, the Son insofar as He is the Redeemer, and the Holy Spirit insofar as He is the Sanctifier.

Has not the power to grasp His majesty?
We have the sacred word of mighty John,
Who witness bears that God cannot be seen.⁴   10
He is the Father, whom no piercing eye
With burning glance has ever yet discerned,
Who put not on the form of man, nor veiled
His Godhead under human mien or mode.
Thou must, blasphemer, spurn the book divine,   15
Or else the Father's might was never seen,
Which cannot mingle with the things of earth.

And yet the Father's image may be seen,
Which has appeared at times to human eyes,
Which our dim sight, though watery and dull,   20
Has had the power through mist and cloud to reach.
Who so of men is said to have seen God
Has seen the Son who is by Him begot;
The Son proceeding from the Father showed
Himself to man in forms that he could grasp.   25
For pure Godhead comes not within our view
Unless it veils itself in earthly form.
This Deity did Abraham behold,
Sire of a noble race and host to Christ,
Who deigned in threefold shape to visit earth.⁵   30
This, too, did Jacob meet with wrestling arms.⁶

The giver of the law divine, himself,
Who, bidden to approach, stood face to face
With God and friendly words exchanged with Him,⁷
Knew that he looked on Christ in fleshly guise.   35
But bolder then, he revelation sought
Not granted unto man and hopeless strove
To see Christ's majesty devoid of flesh.

---
4 Cf. John 1.18; 6.46.
5 Cf. Gen. 18.
6 Cf. Gen. 32.24.
7 Cf. Exod. 33.11

At last, when he had with his present Lord
Conversed at length in easy fellowship,   40
He prayed: 'O gracious Lord, let me know Thee.'[8]
God answered: 'Not myself, but my one Son
The just shall see.'[9] Could He have made more clear
The Word cannot be seen except in earthly form,
That though the Father man cannot behold,   45
The Word may when He wills reveal Himself
To human eyes, and oft assumes the shape
Of man or angel that He may be seen?
It was the Word, breathed from the Father's mouth,
Who of the Virgin took a mortal frame.   50
The human form that not yet in the flesh
Appeared to Moses wore a brow like ours,
Since God, who would by power of the Word
Assume a body, made the face the same.
Flames rose and seemed to burn the thorny bush.[10]   55
God moved amid the branches set with spines,
And tresses of the flames swayed harmlessly,[11]
That He might shadow forth His Son's descent
Into our thorny members sin infests
With teeming briers and fills with bitter woes.   60
For tainted at its root that noxious shrub
Had sprouted from its baneful sap a crop
Of evil shoots beset with many thorns.
The sterile branches suddenly grew bright
As God enkindled with His mighty power   65
The leafy boughs, nor harmed the tangled briers.
He touched the scarlet berries, blood-red fruits,
And grazed the twigs that grew from deadly wood,
For stains of sin are washed away by blood
Shed by the tortured bush with cruel pangs.   70

---

[8] Cf. Exod. 33.13.
[9] Cf. Exod. 33.23.
[10] Cf. Exod. 3.2.
[11] Cf. Vergil, *Aeneid* 2.683.

That seer saw nought but what in flesh was seen,
God's image bright, God's Word, and God the fire[12]
That fills the sinful thorn bush of our frame.
The Source of light and Father of the Word
Exceeds man's sight, as the apostle shows 75
When he denies that Godhead can be seen.[13]
Believe me, no man has seen God, no man.
God sent from heaven may be seen by man,
But not Godhead itself; the One begot
Is visible, not the ingenerate.[14] 80
The Father's mouth is hid, whence came the Son,
Who once revealed Himself, assuming shape
That could the Passion bear, and so required
A human form. For Being infinite
Cannot feel pain, since that celestial fire 85
Stoops not to suffering nor to earthly woes,
But shining, pure, serene, unlimited,
And subject to nought else, it rules all things,
Without beginning, and before all time
The majesty that with the Father dwelt, 90
His spirit and thought, the way of His designs,
Which made not by His hand nor spoken word,
Breathed from the Father's heart, declared His will.[15]

This, then, no scourges rend nor spittle shames;
This no affronting hand torments with blows, 95
Nor sharp and wounding nails fix to a cross.[16]
These racked the human flesh, of Virgin born
By nature's law, without the marriage bond.
Man feels the thirst, man drinks the gall and wine
And shudders at the thought of death and pain.[17] 100

---

12 Cf. Heb. 1.3; Col. 1.15; 1 John 1.5.
13 Cf. John 1.18; 1 John 4.12.
14 Cf. 1 Tim. 6.16.
15 Cf. Ps. 44.1.
16 Cf. Matt. 26.67; 27.26; John 19.1-3.
17 Cf. Matt. 27.34; 26.38,39.

Tell me, you impious teachers, who declare
The Heavenly Father left His throne on high
When God came down into our members frail,
Did, then, the Father suffer? What deceit
Does heresy not dare? Was He conceived,   105
And growing did He swell the Maiden's womb?
And is the page of Holy Scripture false[18]
Which says the Word came forth in form of flesh?[19]
We firmly hold the Father of the Word
Was not made flesh. Stand fast, O Sacred Writ;   110
It suits you not to speak ought false or vague.
The Father none has seen;[20] He never came
To earth, nor bared His light to human eyes.
He sent the Word made visible, and when
He willed, received Him back; the Virgin's womb   115
He by the Word impressed and formed the Child.

God by His power and spirit dwells on earth,
And every part the Father's glory fills;
The Father nowhere absent is, but by
The Word is ever present; hence did Christ   120
To Philip say: 'Am I with you so long,
And you know not the Father seen in Me.'[21]
To the invisible Father it belongs
To generate the visible Son, through whom
The Father can be seen, not by the eyes   125
Of saints alone, but by the sightless orbs
Of darkened souls unmindful of the truth.

If you deny God shows Himself to men,
Tell me whom Babylon's king sees from his throne
Walk through the flames unharmed and firmly tread   130

---
18 Cf. Claudian, *Probino et Olybrio* 197.
19 Cf. John 1.14.
20 Cf. John 6.46.
21 Cf. John 14.9.

The greedy fires that touch not brethren three.[22]
Thus speaks the king: 'This panting furnace, lords,
Received three men into its raging fires,
And, lo, another smiling parts the flames.
It is the Son of God. Him I adore.[23]   135
Remove the brands He scorned, the glowing pine;
The burning brimstone loses now its heat.
The Son it is who works these miracles;[24]
I see Him, God Himself, true Son of God.[25]
He rules the scorching heat, He tames its wrath;   140
He tramples on the yielding fire, He curbs
The blazing pitch and quenches rabid flames.[26]
The torrid blast roars past the strangers' robes,
Commanded not to touch the splendid folds.
Assyrian turbans by the fumes are shunned,   145
Lest flowing locks be soiled by reeking smoke.'[27]
He pauses; then he bids the music cease,
The sackbuts, trumpets, harps, and flutes.
False worship ends and festal notes are hushed
That praised the golden statue he set up.[28]   150
The songs of holy men resounding now
In triple concord laud the heavenly king
Who made the sea, the lands and shining stars[29]
And saved His children in the midst of flames.

To help mankind the Almighty Father's Word   155
Came ever to the earth and out of love
Assumed a human shape, that flesh one day
To be imbued with the eternal Lord
But leading then a fallen, carnal life,

---

22 Cf. Dan. 3.49,50.
23 Cf. Dan. 3.91,92.
24 Cf. Vergil, *Georgics* 4.441.
25 Cf. Vergil, *Aeneid* 6.322.
26 Cf. *ibid.* 5.801-802.
27 Cf. *ibid.* 12.588; Dan. 3.94.
28 Cf. Dan. 3.5.
29 Cf. Dan. 3.51-90.

Might to its Master's image be transformed,[30]　　160
Might know Him sharer of its earthly countenance
The pledge revealed of partnership with Him,
And by degrees draw near its brother Christ.
Man was but carnal once; the Spirit now
Has raised him to the state of heaven's child　　165
By filling him with God's life-giving grace.[31]
A new man now engendered by the Spirit,
But of our substance, from the Virgin drawn,
The primitive corruption has put off
And of Himself put on immortal life;　　170
The Son of Man, but Son of God also,
Alone He looks upon the Father's face.
None knows the Father save the Son and him
To whom the Son, our Savior, makes Him known.[32]
In short, I say, the Father came not down　　175
Into the flesh, but flesh assumed has scaled
The Father's throne; the Son unites them both.

Yield, rash Sabellius, you who scoff at Christ,
Dethrone the Father and deny the Son.
Do you not wrong the Father when you scorn　　180
The Son? No Father He without the Son,[33]
For Him you rob of Son you cannot call
The Father. But perhaps you wish to take
From God a father's love, content to name
Him God, without paternal grace or power.　　185

What pagan lying mid a thousand gods,
Adoring them with salt, incense, and turf,
Deems not a God supreme rules over all?

---

30 *exemplo mutaret eri similesque per artus.* This line, which does not appear in the oldest MSS, is bracketed by Bergman, who regards it as an interpolation.
31 Cf. 1 Cor. 15.45-47.
32 Cf. Matt. 11.27.
33 Cf. Tertullian, *Adversus Praxeam* 10.

Though smoking altars he may consecrate
To Saturn, Juno, her of Cythera,[34]   190
And other monsters, when to heaven he looks,
All sovereignty to one God he refers,
To whom these powers diverse their homage yield.
What tribe so dull of mind or rude of speech,
What heathen cult so sordid as to place   195
The dog Anubis[35] on the heavenly throne?
None gives Cloacina[36] or Epona[37]
A starry seat, though they rank incense pay
And meal and entrails probe with hands profane.[38]
Consult the bearded Plato's wanderings,   200
Consult the musings of the Cynic foul
And Aristotle's knotty arguments.
Though in a maze of dark uncertainty
These go astray,[39] although a hen or cock
They promise, that the god of medicine   205
May deign to favor them at death's approach,
Yet when to norms of reason they conform,
In all their hazy notions, their disputes
And wrangling arguments, they voice belief
In one God by whose power the restless earth   210
Revolves, and wandering stars maintain their course.
Man's nature does not suffer him to doubt
The power supreme, unless he is a brute
And lifts not eyes to heaven with face erect.[40]
Nay, even Numa's soothsayer this divined,   215
And savage Scot, worse than a dog of war.

But we today who twice have seen the Lord,

---

[34] Venus.
[35] An Egyptian deity represented with the head of a dog; cf. Propertius 3.11.41.
[36] A surname of Venus.
[37] A goddess associated with horses; cf. Juvenal 8.157.
[38] Cf. Juvenal 6.551.
[39] Cf. Vergil, *Aeneid* 5.588-591.
[40] Cf. Ovid, *Metamorphoses* 1.86.

In Scripture and in flesh, by faith at first,[41]
Then face to face, who when the cross confirmed
The prophets' words, into His side and hands   220
Our fingers thrust,[42] know Jesus as our King;
And we believe it sinful to deny
The glorious name of Father to our God,
Who from Himself brought forth our King,
King not of Parthian nor of Roman race,[43]   225
But king of worlds above, midway, below,
Lord of creation, King of the universe.
The midmost realm of flesh, the Father's heights,
And Stygian depths He rules. He downward steps
And to Himself returns, is God and man.   230
He dies, but still is God. All human toil
He shares, that He may to the Father bring
Souls that were dead, and raise the body too.
What prophets had foretold to sounding lyres,
We saw and handled, heard His voice and words,[44]   235
And now we understand the seers of old
And prophecies made clear by sight of Christ.

This our salvation is, our life and way,
Never to name the Father without the Son
And never to confess the Son as God   240
Without the Father's name, never invoke
The Father and Son without the Holy Spirit,
Yet not to make of them three separate gods
But understand one God subsists in three.
The Son is not the Father,[45] for we know   245
That of the Unbegot He is true Son
And Father may not be Son to Himself.
It is absurd to think that from Himself

---
41 Cf. Heb. 11.3.
42 Cf. John 20.27.
43 Cf. Vergil, *Georgics* 4.211.
44 Cf. 1 John 1.1.
45 Cf. Tertullian, *op. cit.* 10.

The Father was begot, as some outgrowth
Or new material of a sudden birth;   250
That God brought forth and made Himself this Son.[46]
The names divine express naught vague or false.
The Father is the Father by begetting,
The Son is Son because He is begot.
Coequal with His Father and supreme,   255
How can their operation be the same
Unless the Son has all the Father's might
And in their essence Father and Son are one?

Some further go and this begetting probe,
If it is right for human thought to strive   260
To know this mystery beyond all time,
Beyond all ages and creation's dawn,
Which passes all man's wit to comprehend.[47]
Since origins are difficult to grasp,
How shall to mortal man the power be given   265
To know what God did ere the world began,
How He the Word with no beginning framed?
This is revealed to us: the Word is God,
Of Father unbegot one perfect Son
Without beginning, yet originate,   270
Eternal with the Father, yet born of Him.
The Father was not severed in such way
That part of Him became the Son, nor did
His substance lengthen, dwarfing His Godhead,
As a transmuted portion formed the Son.[48]   275
God changes not, nor does He from Himself
Take anything when He begets the Son,
Who is whole God from whole God, Light from Light.
But when is light without the light? When does
A shining light lack radiance, or when   280

---
[46] Cf. *ibid.* 10,11
[47] Cf. Athanasius, *Oratio contra Arianos* 2.36.
[48] Cf. Hilary, *De Trinitate* 2.22 and 4.4 (Vol. 25, this series).

Does flame diminish flame? When is the Father
And God and Light not God and Father of Light?[49]
If once He was not Father and begot
In time the Son, a new mode He acquired.
Let us not think God's fullness may increase.[50]   285
God and Father, light and glory, He was
For aye, nor was He Father afterwards.
Eternal with the Father Christ we hold,
Begot of Father who no father had.

If, wretch, you doubt the mysteries of Christ's birth,   290
You are not of the Catholic fellowship,
But of the incense bearers, worshipers
Of Deucalions,[51] tombstones, and oiled fig trees.
Nay, in the fountain of antiquity[52]
Seek signs of God, run through the ancient books   295
Of him[53] who did not learn the science of God
From witless sire or boding patriarch,
From hoary tale or prating nurse, or cry
Of noisy crow, but from a gracious God,
Who taught the trembling mortal face to face,[54]   300
Revealing to him all His majesty.
The inspired historian makes it very clear
That at earth's dawn the Father not alone
Nor without Christ His new creation formed.
'God fashioned man,' he says, 'and gave to him   305
The face of God.'[55] What but to say that He
Was not alone, that God stood by God's side
When the Lord made man in image of the Lord?

---

49 Cf. Athanasius, *De decretis Nicenae synod* 23-24; 27; also *Oratio contra Arianos* 2.32.
50 Cf. Hilary, *op. cit.* 3.17 (Vol. 25, this series).
51 Name of several mythological persons, the most important of whom was the son of Prometheus.
52 The Old Testament.
53 Moses, author of the Pentateuch.
54 Cf. Exod. 33.11.
55 Cf. Gen. 1.27.

Christ is the Father's image, we are Christ's;
God made us in the likeness of the Lord,   310
For in our likeness Christ would come in time.
From sacred books, I many texts can cull
To prove, unless you spurn them,⁵⁶ that Godhead
Not only in the Father dwells, but Christ
With Him is God, as Genesis declares:⁵⁷   315
'The Lord rained fire from the Lord on the Sodomites.'
What Lord, and from what Lord, if from His throne
The Father looks alone, or burns with ire?
The Lord the Son hurled down the fiery wrath
Of the Lord the Father; both thunderbolts are one.   320

If listening Jews had so imbibed these truths
That the dull fibers of their hearts were touched,
They would have hearkened to the Lord of heaven
Who had come down to save His wandering sheep,⁵⁸
But all their earrings had been used to mold   325
A head for Baal, and ears of gems were robbed.⁵⁹
From mount of shining light and speech with God
The leader of the sinful race appears
And brings to darkened tents the tables graved
By Hand divine,⁶⁰ but prone the people spurn   330
Christ written in the symbols of the law.⁶¹
Unhappy they, who closed their dazzled eyes
And with enshrouding robes their faces veiled.⁶²
But we with veil flung back see Christ Himself,
And with uncovered face we look on God,⁶³   335
Nor do we lie prostrate beneath the law

---

56 Cf. Vergil, *Georgics* 1.176.
57 Cf. Gen. 19.24.
58 Cf. Matt. 15.24.
59 Cf. Exod. 32.2-4.
60 Cf. Exod. 32.15,16.
61 Cf. 2 Cor. 3.13,14.
62 Cf. Vergil, *Aeneid* 3.545. According to Scripture (Exod. 34.33-35), it was Moses who veiled his face rather than the Israelites.
63 Cf. 2 Cor. 3.18.

But view its splendor with uplifted brow.
Alas for the tree whose boughs were once so fair,
Alas for the olive branch once rich with fruits![64]
Lo with the olive wild engrafted now,   340
Thy stem clothed with strange bark grows green again.
Have pity on thyself. This olive shoot
Boasts not, rejoicing in its foreign stem,
But warns thee, mindful of thy native stock,
To sadden not its leaves with bitter oil   345
Nor envy at thy root its budding crown.[65]
O ingrates, Christ the Lord thou doest blaspheme!

Whose blood, pray tell us, makes your paschal rite
So solemn? Say what yearling lamb is slain.[66]
That lamb is sacred to you every year,   350
But as a beast. It is absurd to deem
It holy with the blood of lambs to smear
The doorposts and to feast on unleavened bread
With merry song, while sin ferments within.
Do you not see, dull men, it is our Pasch   355
You imitate,[67] and that these old-law rites
Prefigure all the Passion's Mystery,
That Passion which the forehead signs with blood
Upon the dwelling of our body smeared.[68]
This sign the wild Egyptian tempest flees,[69]   360
This shakes the deadly rule of Pharian king,
This Abraham with all his faithful race
Saves from the hail that falls on heathen power.[70]
The son of Abraham upon his brow
Bears marks of blood and has through faith   365
Seen God on earth, true God of the Father born.

---
64 Vergil, *Georgics* 2.31 and 81.
65 Cf. Rom. 11.17,18.
66 Cf. Exod. 12.5,6.
67 Cf. 1 Cor. 5.7,8.
68 Cf. Exod. 12.7,23.
69 Cf. Exod. 10.13.
70 Cf. Exod. 9.23-25.

When Abraham saw God, he trusted Him,
But you, his carnal sons, look on all things
With carnal eyes and by a spiritual law
Do works of flesh, for not from heaven came   370
The fleshly law you heed, but one Christ fills,
Engendering hope. What hope but light divine,
The Lord's advent first seen by Abraham
And promised by the Father to our eyes
In time to come, by word of the law confirmed?   375
Not only of the law. What writers now
Are not intent on Christ, or what bookcase
Lacks recent tomes that laud Christ's wondrous works?
The Hebrew pen, the fluent style of Greece,
And Latin eloquence give praise to Him.   380
Unwitting, Pilate gave command: 'Go, scribe,
Write in three tongues what might is crucified,'[71]
A threefold title on the gibbet's head,
That reading it, Judaea may know God,
And Greece and golden Rome may worship Him.   385
The trumpet's blare from hollow horn of brass,
Sweet hymns the potent breath pours from the heart,
The vibrant notes of sacred harp and lyre,
The blended harmonies of organ reeds,
And songs of shepherds rival glens repeat,   390
All join in praising Christ, in singing Christ,
And mute things speak of Christ, moved by these strains.

O Name most sweet, my light and grace and hope,[72]
My refuge sure! O certain rest from toil,[73]
Sweet savor, fragrant perfume, living spring,   395
Chaste love, resplendent beauty, true delight.
If deaf, that race will not incline its ears
To hear Thy praise, which myriad voices

---

[71] Cf. John 19.19,20.
[72] Cf. Horace, *Odes* 1.1.2.
[73] Cf. Vergil, *Aeneid* 3.393.

In all the earth with such great joy announce,
Then let it listen to the frenzied cries   400
The fiend pours forth from hearts he has possessed[74]
And put its faith in them: Apollo writhes,
Struck by the name of Christ, nor can he bear
The Word's fierce lightning flash; the lashing tongue[75]
That lauds Christ's wondrous works torments the wretch.   405
God's priest intones: 'Fly, crafty serpent, fly!
Go out of him and loose your hidden coils.
The man you vex, foul thief, belongs to Christ.
Have done, Christ present guards his mortal frame!
You may not seize as prey one joined to Christ.   410
Away, proud spirit, Christ bids you go from him!'
At this the fierce Cyllenian god laments,
And Jupiter exhales his well-known fires.
Behold, a legion hurls headlong the swine
Of Gerasenes, and once enchained in tombs,   415
It loudly grunts with pain. From lips possessed
It had cried out: 'O Jesus, Son of God,
Offspring of David's royal line, we know
Who Thou art and why Thou hast come, what power
Expels us, at Thy coming filled with dread.'[76]   420

Has not this voice, Judaea, reached your ears?[77]
True, but it has not pierced your darkened mind
And, driven back, has from the threshold fled.
The man where sets the evening sun, and he
Who first beholds the rosy dawn has heard   425
Of the Lord's advent. The fervent Gospel word
Has thawed the Scythian frosts and Hyrcanian snows,
So that Rhodopeian Hebrus, freed from ice,
Flows from Caucasian cliffs, a gentler stream.
The Getans mild have grown; Gelonians now   430

---
74 Cf. Mark 1.23,24.
75 Cf. Horace, *Odes* 3.12.3.
76 Cf. Mark 5.1-13; Luke 8.26-33.
77 Cf. Vergil, *Georgics* 3.461-463.

Their bloody thirst allay with cups of milk,
Henceforth to drink the sacred blood of Christ.[78]
The realm of Afric Atlas, once infidel,
At Christian altars crowns its bearded kings.
Since God, the Spirit, touched a mortal womb,   435
And with His Mother's flesh God clothed Himself,
Since from Virginity He was made man,
The Delphic cave is hushed, its omens damned,
The tripod boding nought, and panting priest
No fates from Sibylline pages hissing forth;   440
False Dodona has lost its raging fumes,
Dumb Cumae mourns its oracles, now dead,
And from Libyan deserts Ammon speaks no more.
The Roman capitol mourns to see its chiefs
Own Christ as God and her temples fall   445
At their command. Aeneas' royal heir
Kneels as a suppliant in the house of Christ
And venerates the standard of the cross.

Yet in my youth there was an emperor,[79]
As I remember well, one brave in war,   450
A wise lawgiver, famed in word and deed,
Who held our country dear but not our faith,
For he adored at shrines of many gods.
Unfaithful to God, though faithful to the world,
Before Minerva's throne he bent his head,   455
A plaster Juno's sandals kissed, at the feet
Of Hercules he knelt, Diana's knees
He smeared with wax, and at Apollo's shrine
He crouched or entrails burned to Pollux's horse.[80]
Once he was offering bloody sacrifice   460
To Hecate; the cattle stood in line
Awaiting the pontiff's ax, and somber wreaths

---
78 Allusion to the Eucharist.
79 Julian the Apostate (361-363).
80 Cf. Vergil, *Aeneid* 6.254.

Of cypress round the heifers' horns were twined.
And now the aged priest with chaplet crowned
Had thrust his knife into a victim's breast, 465
And as with bloody hands the veins he held
And the pulse was counting with augural skill
Until the heart, still warm, would cease to beat,
He suddenly grew pale and cried aloud:
'What do I here? A greater power, O King, 470
I know not what, has marred our sacrifice,
Greater than bowls of foaming milk can bear,[81]
Or blood of cattle slain and herbs and crowns.
I see the shades I summoned scattered far;
Persephone affrighted turns away[82] 475
And flees with torch put out and scourge withdrawn.
No cryptic murmur, no Thessalian charm,
Nor victim can recall the banished spirits.
Do you not see the flames in censers droop,
And embers slowly turn to ashen gray? 480
The royal servant cannot hold the cup,
And balsams trickle from his feeble hand;
The bays slip from the startled flamen's head,
The victim thwarts the aim of wavering steel.
Some Christian has crept hither unawares; 485
The band and couch divine this race abhor.
Let him by water and by chrism signed[83]
Depart, and let Proserpine return.'
He spoke, and bloodless fell; the prince himself,
As though he saw Christ's threatening thunderbolt, 490
Grew pale, and putting off his royal crown,
Looked round those standing near to see what youth
Signed with the holy symbol of the cross

---
81 Cf. *ibid*. 3.66.
82 Cf. *ibid*. 10.646.
83 Reference to Christian baptism and confirmation; cf. Lactantius, *Div. inst.* 4.27 (Vol. 49, this series).

Had muddled Zoroaster's magic spells.[84]
An armor-bearer from the royal guard   495
Of fair-haired youths was seized, who, throwing down
His double-headed spears with jewels set,
Acknowledged that he bore the sign of Christ.
The prince uprose, and banishing the priest,
He fled in terror from the marble fane;   500
The trembling guards, unmindful of their lord,
Look up to heaven and to Jesus pray.

Judaea, do you not deplore your crime?
Lo, Christ your God your Sabbath has annulled
And raised man to a Sabbath infinite.   505
He has shone forth on nations and on kings;
He rules the world, and mighty Rome has forced
To yield her false Tarpeian gods to Him.
Learn from your bitter woes, unhappy race,
Who smites your vain beliefs and carnal laws,   510
Who tramples on you with avenging power.
Do not the quarried stones of Solomon
Now lie in ruins, that temple built by hand?[85]
Why so? The mortal hand of mason wrought
That short-lived work. It rightly lies in ruins,   515
Since every work of art returns to nought.
All that is made is doomed one day to fall.
Learn what our temple is, if you would know;[86]
It is one that no artisan has built,
A structure not of riven fir or pine,   520
Nor reared with blocks of quarried marble fair.
Its massive weight no columns high support
Beneath the arches of a gilded vault.
By God's Word it was formed, not by His voice,

---

[84] Julian the Apostate had revived the cult of Mithras, the origin of which had been attributed to the Persian lawgiver, Zoroaster.
[85] Cf. Acts 7.47,48.
[86] Cf. Heb. 8.2.

But by the everlasting Word, the Word made flesh.[87]   525
This temple is eternal, without end,
This you attacked with scourge and cross and gall.
This temple was destroyed by bitter pains.[88]
Its form was fragile from the Mother's womb,
But when brief death the Mother's part dissolved,   530
The Father's might restored it in three days.
You have beheld my saving temple rise
On high, surrounded by an angel throng.[89]
The everlasting gates[90] uphold its roof;
Through lofty towers the glorious stairs arise,   535
And at the top appears a shining path.
Your offerings lie beneath a heap of ruins.
What judgment you deserve Titus has taught,
And Pompey, too; by their cohorts dispersed[91]
Your race is borne through every land and sea.   540
The Jew in exile wanders far and wide
Since he was banished from his fatherland,
And stained with blood of Christ, whom he denied,
Has paid the penalty his crime deserved.
See how the ancient virtue has declined!   545
The noble heir of the faithful patriarchs
Has been enslaved and is an outcast now.
The thrall adopts the faith of recent times,
So great its power. Confessing Christ, a race
Once infidel prevails, but subject now   550
To faithful lords, is that which doubted Christ.

Some heretics a doctrine teach, akin
To Jewish rage, and follow Christ halfway.[92]
That He is truly man, this they affirm,

---
87 Cf. John 1.14.
88 Cf. Mark 14.58; John 2.19-21.
89 Cf. Acts 1.10.
90 Cf. Ps. 23.7.
91 Pompey took Jerusalem in 63 B.C., and Titus destroyed the city in 70 A.D.
92 The Ebionites, early Christian sects infected with Judaistic errors.

But not that He is God from heaven come. 555
They own His virtue, but His power deny:
His life they praise, His Godhead take away.
The mighty work that shows both skill and power
Is born of genius or of virile strength:
One fruit of mind, the other of brute force. 560
Both mortal are in man; for mind with age
Grows weak, and time exhausts the strongest arms.
This we believe not of the eternal power
And glory of the Lord; we hold He springs
Not from the seed of earth nor from man's sin; 565
A heavenly fire engenders Him, not flesh
Nor blood of father, nor impure desire.[93]
By power of God a spotless maid conceives,
As in her virgin womb the Spirit breathes.
The mystery of this birth confirms our faith 570
That Christ is God: a maiden by the Spirit
Is wed, unstained by love; her purity
Remains intact; with child within, untouched
Without, bright in her chaste fertility,
Mother yet virgin, Mother that knew not man.[94] 575
Why, doubter, do you shake your silly head?
An angel makes this known with holy lips.[95]
Will you not hearken to angelic words?
The Virgin blest, the shining messenger
Believed, and by her faith she Christ conceived. 580
Christ comes to men of faith and spurns the heart
Irresolute in trust and reverence.
The Virgin's instant faith attracted Christ
Into her womb and hid Him there till birth.
Believe what says the angel who was sent 585
From the Father's throne, or if your stolid ear
Catch not the voice from heaven, be wise and hear

---
[93] Cf. John 1.13.
[94] Cf. Luke 1.34.
[95] Cf. Luke 1.30-33.

POEMS 25

The cry of aged woman, now with child.⁹⁶
O wondrous faith! The babe in senile womb
Greets through his Mother's lips the Virgin's Son,   590
Our Lord; the child unborn makes known the cry
Of the Child bestowed on us,⁹⁷ for speechless yet,
He caused that mouth to herald Christ as God.
Give me the prophecies, unroll the book
That God inspired Isaia to bring forth: 595
I love to read and ponder on the lines
That golden hand in flaming letters wrote.
Go hence, as the bright symbols I adore
And weeping print fond kisses on the words;⁹⁸
My joy gives rise to tears, joy makes them flow.   600
The promised day that verse foretold has come,⁹⁹
On which a Virgin Mother bore a Child,
With faithful witness of her anxious spouse,¹⁰⁰
And gave me sight of my Emmanuel.
Is not this God now ours? With us as man   605
Abiding, He confirms this name and makes
The ancient scripture by His presence clear.

Is He not God whose crib the East adores,
On golden salvers offering regal gifts
To the swaddled Babe upon the Virgin's knee?¹⁰¹   610
What herald swifter than the southern wind
Announced to peoples of the Bactrian lands
The joyous dawn on which the Infant Christ¹⁰²
Hung on the breast of His Mother undefiled?
'We saw this Child borne through the stars,' they said, 615
'Far brighter than the path of ancient signs.'¹⁰³

---
96 Cf. Luke 1.42-45.
97 Cf. Isa. 9.6.
98 Cf. Vergil, *Aeneid* 1.687.
99 Cf. Isa. 7.14.
100 Cf. Matt. 1.18-22.
101 Cf. Matt. 2-11.
102 Cf. Vergil, *Georgics* 2.337.
103 Cf. Matt. 2.2.

A watcher on Chaldaean peaks at night
Shuddered to see the Serpent disappear,
The Lion flee, the Crab draw mangled feet
Against his side, the vanquished Bull bemoan   620
His broken horns, and sheared Goat fade away.
Here vanishes the Water-bearer, there
The Arrows, Twins bewildered stray apart,
The Maid untrue forsakes her silent loves,
And other fires that hang in frightful clouds   625
Have trembled at the new-born Morning Star.
The sun's pale car stands still, as he foresees
That near eclipse, when veiled at noon his light
Would be obscured in sable night by day,
And earth in sudden gloom would hide its head.[104]   630
Shall I not load this Child with gifts of myrrh,
Incense, and gold? I know Him, what I owe.
Shall I not worship Him beheld in sky
And found on earth, who rules as king and God
Both realms, who by His death hell's reign dissolves 635
And bids the buried rise and follow Him?[105]
He dwells in heaven, sojourns on earth, invades
The depths of hell. True faith this: He is God,
Who is wholly everywhere.[106] Did idle dream
Or word mislead those seers? Did they by chance   640
Bring futile gifts or offer homage blind?
What reason prompted them to bow their heads
At Mary's feet or at the infant's crib
If he was only man, and almighty power
Filled not his tender frame with breath divine?   645

Let pass the Magi, incense, gold, and myrrh,
All showing Him true God, the manger, bands,
His mother's bosom blest, bright from the star:

---

[104] Cf. Luke 23.44,45.
[105] Cf. Matt. 27.52,53.
[106] Cf. Augustine, *Epist.* 187.14 (Vol. 30, this series).

His power and miracles proclaim Him God.
I see the wild winds suddenly grow calm 650
When Christ commands;[107] I see the storm-tossed sea
Grow smooth, with tranquil surface bright,
At Christ's behest; I see the waves grow firm
As the raging flood sustains His treading feet.
He walks dry-shod upon the flowing tide 655
And bears upon the flood with footsteps sure.[108]
He chides the winds and bids the tempest cease.[109]
Who would command the stormy gales: 'Be still,
Your strongholds keep and leave the boundless sea,'
Except the Lord and Maker of the winds? 660
The snowy north wind and the eastern squalls
Yield to the Lord of clouds and Ruler of storms[110]
And sweep the tempest from the smiling sky.
Who on the sea could walk, who with firm step
Upon the flood could without sinking tread 665
That path with soles upborne and feet unwet,
Except the Author of the deep, the Spirit,
Poured from the Father's lips, that moved across
The waves,[111] not yet hemmed in by solid shores?
As servant of its Lord, the sea sustained 670
His step, becoming firm beneath His feet.

Why dwell upon Christ's wondrous works as God?
You who His Godhead doubt, but own Him man,
Observing them, will own that He is God.
Clay with His sacred spittle mixed He smeared[112] 675
On blinded eyes and sight with mud restored:
The night of blindness found a cure in clay,
And moistened earth dispelled the sightless gloom.

---

107 Cf. Matt. 8.23-27.
108 Cf. John 6.19.
109 Cf. Mark 4.39.
110 Cf. Vergil, *Aeneid* 1.80.
111 Cf. Gen. 1.2.
112 Cf. John 9.6.

He showed the man a pool wherein to wash
His grime away. Siloe gushes forth[113] 680
From time to time, not in continuous flow,
And fills the pool brimful at intervals.
The ailing throngs sigh for the grudging spring,
Waiting to bathe sore limbs in the crystal pool.
Upon the banks they lie, intent to hear 685
The noisy outpour from the dripping rocks.
Christ bids the man in this pure spring wash off
The clay,[114] and seeing new lights up his face.
He knew that He from slime had shaped a form,
Once dark, and healing from His lips had shed 690
On the new Adam He had made before.
Without the breath divine of the Lord on high
Our earth was dry, not ripe for healing art,
But since the Spirit from God's mouth bedewed
The Virgin's soil, it is redeemable. 695
Thence it draws sap, the saving unction spread,
And light baptismal waters then infuse.
The blind man, eyes now opened by Christ's mouth,
Cries that the clay and water gave him sight
And through the wondering towns the Author owns, 700
The Author of the light and of the days,
Who in His body showed to sinful man
The cleansing virtue of the healing flood.

Of myriad works the world could not contain[115]
I shall tell briefly of a very few. 705
Five loaves and fishes two He orders placed[116]
As food before the people thronging round
Their Master, by their hunger undeterred,
Who mindful not of food forgot their towns,

---
[113] Cf. John 5.2,3,7.
[114] Prudentius considers the pool of Siloe the same as the pool of Bethsaida (John 5.2).
[115] Cf. John 21.25.
[116] Cf. Mark 6.38-44.

Their forts, their markets, hamlets, trading posts, 710
And cities, glad to feed upon His words.
The festive gathering swarms upon the plain;
By hundreds they recline in friendly bands,
And round the countless boards they range themselves
To dine on two small fish and scanty crusts 715
He multiplies—know now that He is God!
The banquet ended, plates still overflow,
And with the crumbs twelve baskets then they fill;
The rude swain strives with undigested fare,
The waiter groans beneath his heavy load. 720
Who can a great feast spread from viands few?
Who but the Maker of our frame and all
That nurtures it, who shaped the world from nought?
Almighty God without the aid of seed
Fashioned the earth, not as the sculptor dowers 725
With life the block of bronze from metal fused.
All that now is was nought: that nothingness
Was into being brought and bidden grow.
Small was the first creation, but it grew
Till it became the mighty universe. 730
Therefore, when I behold that meager fare
Thus multiplied within the hands of Christ,
Can I doubt that the elemental forms
First made by Him from nothing, by degrees
Have grown to that perfection we now see? 735
Lest fragments should be trodden on and lost,
When men had fed, or should become the spoil
Of wolves or foxes or of petty mice,
Twelve men were charged to heap in baskets full[117]
The gifts of Christ to keep and spread afar. 740

But why do I, unworthy as I am,
With quavering voice sing these holy deeds?
Come, Lazarus, from the tomb and say whose voice

---
[117] Allusion to the twelve apostles.

You heard in depths of earth, what fiat pierced
The dark abode of death, so that when Christ 745
Bids you return to life, you heed His word,
As though near by, and rise without delay![118]
What gulf so nigh joins to the living world
The neighboring realm of shades? Where is the cave
That plunges downward into vasty hell, 750
The river rolling fire 'tween banks unfilled?
Before the entrance to the tomb, closed fast
By monstrous stones set in the tunneled rock,
The Lord stands still and calls His dead friend's name.
Then lo, as stones roll back, the loathsome grave 755
Gives up the living bones, a walking corpse.
Loose now, you joyful sisters, fragrant bands!
The only odor there exhaled is scented balm,
And breezes do not waft corruption's stench.
Eyes freed from oozing matter glow again 760
With bygone luster; by degrees the cheeks
Once putrefied take on a rosy hue.
Who could imbue the crumbling frame with life?
He only, who the body gave, who breathed
The living soul into the molded clay, 765
From whom the slime received its sanguine bloom.
O death, grown docile to authority,
O death, once deaf, now taught to hear commands,
Who has such mastery over you? Confess
Jesus who wrests me from you to be God. 770
Take those who Christ deny, none hinders you;
Use power alloted you, in endless night,
To hold blasphemers. Captive now, release
The just, who know that Christ is God and man,
That highest God put on our mortal flesh. 775
He takes the form He shaped, nor thinks it shame
To wear it. Body and living soul I mean.
With hands He made the body, the soul He breathed

---
[118] Cf. John 11.43,44.

From His own lips. The whole man God assumes,
Wholly from Him; the whole man He redeems,[119]   780
The body from the tomb, the soul from hell.

Comes now a doubting casuist, who inquires:
'Is it of faith to hold that the breath of God,
Our soul, can suffer torment, that it goes
To deepest hell and there is burned by fire?'   785
Believe not that the soul is God, but that,
Though greater than all things, it too was made.
By God's mouth it was shaped and existed not
Before, but was created fair in form,
Endowed with grace divine and filled with God,   790
Like to its Maker, yet not God itself,
For not begotten, it God's creature is;
The Son alone came from the Father's heart,
True God. The soul that was not, being gained.
The Son is coeternal with the Father,   795
Ever in Him;[120] not made but born, He has
All that the Father has, whereas the soul
Is but God's image. Thus its Maker spoke
When He in His own likeness man designed.[121]
The image but reflects reality,   800
The image of the truth is not the truth.
The soul is like to God, for it is not
Consumed by time; wise and inclined to good,
It rules the world as queen, it sees before,
It plans, takes heed and speaks, makes words and laws,   805
Is skilled in arts and roams the heavens in thought.[122]
Thus God has made the soul like to Himself;
All else He made unlike. For what has bounds
Can be discerned with ease, but God on high

---

119 Cf. Rom. 8.11; Col. 1.22.
120 Cf. John 1.1,2.
121 Cf. Gen. 1.26.
122 Cf. Wisd. 7.22-24.

Who fills the world[123] has in Him nought finite   810
That human thought can grasp or entertain.
That power cannot be fathomed which is limitless
And fills the reaches of unmeasured space.
The foul corruption of the flesh receives
The soul, which is created and is less   815
Than God, but greater than all creatures else,
With power o'er all, and the tainted body shares
Its own defilement with the soul at birth.
Our sinful clay then mingles with pure spirit.
You may deny the soul was formed or made   820
Since from the Lord's mouth it has flowed, as if
A part of God could be defiled with sin
And be condemned to hell (a crime to say).
It is of God, I grant, yet what in time
Began may not be called a part of God,   825
Nor prior to the body deemed to live.
It was created when the friendly heart
It entered as a sister, taking up
Its dwelling with its brother, new-formed clay.
It is indeed the breath of God, but not   830
His essence whole, breathed forth with that control
Which He who breathed determined to maintain.
We cannot gaze into the depths of God,[124]
But man of Deity the mirror is.[125]
We incorporeal being may discern   835
Though Christ, who showed the Father in His flesh.[126]
Mark how diverse are vapors we exhale
When from our lips the breath of air we blow.
Now torrid breath a current warm emits
And pours forth humid clouds from moistened throats;   840
Now, when we please, the airy breath comes forth
Like chilling wind and makes a whistling sound.

---
[123] Cf. Wisd. 1.7.
[124] Cf. Wisd. 9.13; 1 Cor. 2.16.
[125] Cf. Wisd. 7.26.
[126] Cf. John 14.9,10.

Add, too, the varied breath the flute imbibes:
Now feeble, rendering the tone subdued,
Now with strong blasts producing swelling notes; 845
It loudly rends the air or faintly sighs;
With scanty breath indrawn it makes shrill sounds,
Or a low murmur gently presses out.

When this in mortal body you can do,
Why should you not believe the eternal God 850
Could into man infuse what soul He willed?
And since within set bounds He breathed it forth,
It must have been created. While our soul
Knows many things, it reaches not to all.
Since it is finite and omniscience lacks, 855
It is created; cause and source it had.
Learn from a likeness whether it is made.
The hand of God the human body formed,
His fingers shaped the clay.[127] But does this mean
The hand of God has joints? Has it a palm? 860
Do fingers close or open wide at will?
Our hand is fashioned thus; no hand like this
The Lord unbounded has, but we to Him
Ascribe a form the human mind can grasp.
As He is said the body to have shaped 865
In a corporeal way, so the spirit of man,
Formed by ethereal breath, is said to be
The work of His mouth, through which the soul flashed forth,
Aware that it was made with finite powers.
If of His hand our flesh is not the work, 870
Then neither is our soul, caused by His breath
And lodged in its proper seat, work of His mouth.
All things brought forth in time have fixed abode,
And what is held in narrow bounds is small,
Not everywhere diffused; what is so small 875
As to be set in space, unstable is

---
127 Cf. Gen. 2.7.

And subject to corruption; the corrupt
Has hell deserved; such being is not God.
Or if the soul is divine, what means the grace
New-poured into the soul deprived of Christ, 880
Which by baptism justified, the Spirit
Adorns as God's handmaid with further light?
Since grace is given or denied by worth,
To say the soul is God or part of God
Is nonsense, for it freely drinks this grace, 885
Then loses it by sin and crime; now yields
To punishment, then treads it under foot.

Does it surprise you that the soul can sin,
Which in a house of flesh was made to dwell,
When the very angel sins[128] who tarries not 890
In fragile mortal frame? He sins for he
Was made and not begot; how so the Lord
Who made him knows. Enough that I believe.
The world's Creator alone is free from sin,[129]
The unbegotten and begotten God, 895
The Father and Son. Alone exempt from pain,
He lives untouched and knows no bitterness.
Say that the soul is free from cross and woes,
If you have found it free from sin and crime.
The being that can sin can suffer pain. 900
Untarnished when created was the soul
That mingling with our clay caused it to live,
For primal shape it took from source divine
And of celestial brightness it was born,
But joined to heavy earth and too much charmed 905
By sweet allurements, its first fervor cooled,
And in the mire it soiled its precious flame
By spurning and transgressing God's decrees.
Such was the soul's first state. Created pure,

---

128 Cf. Job 4.18; 2 Peter 2.4.
129 Cf. 2 Cor. 5.21; 1 John 3.5.

Through sordid union with the flesh it fell 910
Into iniquity; stained by Adam's sin,
It tainted all the race from him derived,[130]
And infant souls inherit at their birth
The first man's sin; not one is sinless born.
But we must shun the false belief that souls 915
To offspring are transmitted with the flesh,
As blood to veins formed by the parent stock.
Souls breed not souls, but nature operates
In unknown ways to make the vessels breathe
And to the whole the spark of life impart. 920
A new soul each new body permeates,
But since it is not cleansed from ancient stain,
In the sin of our first parents, it is old.
Then nature's soil is laved in the second birth,
When by baptism we are born again, 925
And the old Adam our fair soul puts off.[131]
Joined to the body, it finds cause of sin
In promptings of the flesh and also leads
Its comrade into sin; hence vengeful fire
Embraces both the culprits and subjects 930
To equal torments the associates in crime.

Christ frees us from these torments, who was born
Of sinless mother and sinless body wore.
Jesus assumed a nature exposed to pain,
But not to sin's contagion; undefiled 935
And free from guile and every trace of sin,
He, therefore, owed no debt to punishment.[132]
Could punishment that follows sin affect
Christ's body? Could death, where human sin is not?
Vain and impotent would their efforts be 940
For sin in Him no fuel would supply.

---
130 Cf. Rom. 5.12.
131 Cf. Eph. 4.22-24.
132 In two MSS the following line is inserted here: *quid peccatorum prosapia corpore in illo.*

Death feeds on sin; the one who has no sin
Slays death made weak by lack of sustenance.[133]
Thus in Christ's body death was nullified,
Thus did it perish from lack of wonted food. 945
Adore divinity immune from sin,
The nature of the Father and of Christ;
Cease to excite ill-will against our soul
By saying it is God or part of God;
To cut a part from Christ or God is wrong 950
Or to decrease the Godhead, ever whole.

We must expose the doctrine dark and vague[134]
Composed of subtle atoms closely joined,
Which empty falls and fades away like wind
And lacking substance quickly disappears. 955
The Manichaean says a phantom God
Without real body flitted round, a shade
With hollow form and nothing tangible.
But first consider whether aught unreal
Should be ascribed to God, whose glory pure 960
Admits no fraud. Would He array Himself
With members false, pretending to be man
And lying when He said: 'Deep-seated ills
I cure and sins forgive; the Son of Man
Has power to cast out disease of flesh, 965
To loose and break the bonds of wickedness;
Arise, now hale, arise now innocent,
Take up thy bed, I Son of Man command'?[135]
Does He not know Himself and His own flesh?
When His disciples truly He forewarned 970
What sufferings the Son of Man would bear,[136]

---
[133] Cf. Rom. 6.22,23.
[134] In lines 952-1084, the poet condemns the heresy of the Docetists, who taught that the humanity of Christ was an illusion. Various forms of Docetism were current among the Gnostics and the Manichaeans.
[135] Cf. Matt. 9.2-6.
[136] Cf. Matt. 26.2.

Did He not own Himself to be true man
With all His Father's power? If this I doubt,
They were deceived. Would you God's essence know,
O Manichaean, He is truth; if false, 975
He is not God: God's dealings are not false.
You bring against the eternal God the charge
That He has come to us in spurious form.
Be silent, madman; bite your tongue, base dog!
Devour your words with lacerated mouth. 980
Matthew defies your barkings, stems your rage
For he records the human lineage[137]
Of Christ incarnate, reckoning the names
Of six times seven men and tracing the course
Of noble blood through His ancestral line. 985
Christ came the seventh cycle to complete
By adding to the sixth the number that brings
The year of peace, when various bonds are loosed
And mankind is redeemed from human death.[138]
For then imperfect was our mortal clay, 990
But Jesus comes the only perfect man
In whom the seven sevens were complete
That crowned the human race with endless worth.
The seventh sabbath He fulfills for us,
That joined at last to God, our flesh may rest,[139] 995
Which for six sabbaths bore the wounds of sin.
Let us the known succession scan and trace
The line of kings: you will discern that Christ
From human forebears came, of David's seed
And of his blood accounted as an heir. 1000
What say you of the sacred words of Luke
When he the genealogy repeats,[140]
The fleshly line retracing through old sires?

---

[137] Cf. Matt 1.1-17.
[138] An allusion to the Jewish year of jubilee which followed seven cycles of seven years; cf. Lev. 25.8-10.
[139] Cf. Heb. 4.9.
[140] Cf. Luke 3.23-38.

Up generations seventy and two
Christ mounts—so many teachers into the world 1005
He sent—and by the steps down to His birth
Goes back to Adam, head of earthly flesh.
The Father then receives His Son and us,
And Adam son of God becomes through Christ.[141]
Nought now remains but that you deem this race 1010
Unreal, Levi, Juda, Simeon,
King David, other mighty kings, unreal,
The virgin's swelling womb itself grown big
With lying vapor, flimsy clouds, and mist;
That airy blood dissolves, the bones grow soft 1015
And melt, the trembling muscles disappear;
That every deed the idle wind dispels,
The breezes scatter, all an empty tale.

If Christ my nature takes not on Himself,
What does He do? Whom does He free from sin, 1020
If he disdains or shrinks from flesh He made?
Is He ashamed to wear an earthly form
Who did not take it ill to handle clay[142]
When once He made our body out of slime,
Not flesh as yet, but viscid lump of mire, 1025
And molded with His thumb our mortal frame?
Such love of earth,[143] such love of us He has,
He deigns to grasp the fertile clod of soil
With hands divine, nor deems it base to touch
The slimy mass. Command He gave that light 1030
Be made; as He commanded it was made.[144]
All things came into being at His word;
Man only merited to take his form
From the Lord's own hand, born of God's workmanship.
Why has our clay been favored with such love 1035

---
[141] Cf. Luke 3.38.
[142] Cf. Gen. 2.7.
[143] Cf. Vergil, *Georgics* 2.301.
[144] Cf. *ibid.* 1.3.

That by the hands of the Lord it should be shaped,
Blessed by His skill, ennobled by His touch?
God willed that Christ be joined to spotless clay;
Hence He held worthy what He deigned to mold
With sacred hands and make His dearest Son.   1040
Our weakened nature lost the shapely form
Of molded earth and fell a prey to death,
But God's eternal nature willed to assume
Our fragile clay, first tainted by our use,
That it might be corruptible no more.   1045
Christ is our flesh; He dies, He rises for me;[145]
I die, and by Christ's power I rise again.
When Christ is dead and is entombed with tears,
I see myself; when from the grave He comes,
I see my God. If of my body He   1050
A phantom is, He is a phantom of God;
In both Christ must be false, if Christ can feign.
If He is not true man, proved by His death,
He is not the true God His works declare.
Believe He died or doubt He rose again,   1055
And on two grounds deny that Christ is real.
If Jesus did not die and rise again,
Where is divinity? God's might appears
When, dead and buried, He returns to life.
Whoever says that Christ is God must say   1060
That He is man, or rob Godhead of power.
I know my body will arise in Christ:
Why bar my hope? I shall return by paths
He trod in conquering death; this we believe.
Whole I shall rise; renewed, not less than now   1065
Nor otherwise: my face, my strength, my hue,
The same will be; the tomb will give me up
Without the loss of even tooth or nail.
He who bids me return, nought weak will raise;

---

145 Cf. Rom. 4.24,25; 1 Cor. 15.22.

If corruption rise, resurgence there is none.[146]   1070
What trial has snatched from me, what plague or pain
Has worn away, what wasting age cut off,
All will my risen body join again.
For vanquished death should nothing maimed give back
From defrauding grave, though bodies it devoured   1075
Were maimed already; but disease and pain
Were death's domain; what piecemeal it consumed,
It will give back somehow, so that the dead
Will rise with bodies undeformed and whole.
O banish fear, my body, and believe   1080
That you with Christ, our God, will rise, for He
Is clothed with you and calls you back with Him.
Laugh at disease, defy misfortune's blows,
Despise the tomb. Go, where Christ risen calls!

---

146 Cf. 1 Cor. 15.42,43.

THE ORIGIN OF SIN

(HAMARTIGENIA)

THE ORIGIN OF SIN

Preface

Two brothers, one a yoeman and a shepherd one,[1]
The first offspring of her who was of women first,
From fruits of their own labors on the altar place
The firstlings to be offered as a gift to God.
One offers fruits of earth, one living creature gives;   5
Competing in their diverse gifts, they immolate
The one a lamb, the other produce of his fields.
God looked with favor on the younger's sacrifice
But frowned upon the offering by the elder brought.
Hark, from the heavenly throne a mighty voice sounds: 10
'Be silent, Cain; for if you rightly offer gifts,[2]
But you divide them not according to just rule,
Your impious offering becomes a grievous fault.'
The elder brother, jealous of the virtue blessed,
Then arms his bloody hand and with his weeding hook   15
He strikes and cruelly breaks his younger brother's neck.
By this unhallowed crime he stained the new-formed world,
To be made clean in its declining years
By the sacred blood of Christ, which overcame the fiend.
With wounding of the innocent, death first began,   20
And when the sinless One was struck, it ceased to be;
In sin it had its origin, in sin it fell,
For Abel it destroyed first, then struck down Christ,
And met its end by wounding One who has no end.
The ancient story thus foreshadowed things to come;   25

---
1 Cf. Gen. 4.2-5.
2 Cf. Gen. 4.7, according to the Septuagint; also Ambrose, *De Cain et Abel* 2.6 (Vol. 42, this series).

The latest slaying was prefigured by the first,
When that rude countryman who sowed the seeds of death,
Upon the altar placing homely fruits of earth
And deeming God the God of dead and lifeless things,
In his black envy of the living offering   30
Thought meet for sacrifice crops dug from earth with spades.
I see the one of whom this figure is a type,
The heartless fratricide, the jealous murderer,
Who basely rends the form of sacrificial rites
And thinks that he more justly offers vows to God.   35
Marcion[3] it is, a creature of the vilest clay,
Who sows a doctrine of two Gods, against the Spirit,
Presenting gifts of flesh impure and stained with guilt,
And worshiping the eternal God in separate forms.
If he would silence keep and mind the warning voice,   40
The Christian body would enjoy unruffled peace
In worship of one living God of living things.
Devoting all his being to an empty creed,
He impiously divides the sovereign Deity;
Distinguishing the bad and good as separate realms   45
Of two Godheads, he entrusts to them these scepters twain,
Believing to be God one he as evil owns.
He is a bloody Cain, abhorring unity,
A cultivator of the world, foul murderer,
Whose sacrifice is vile and savors of the earth,   50
The earth of man's decaying body, putred clay
Composed of muddy water mingled with the dust
That flowers by nature in luxuriant wickedness,
Engendering the myriad crimes of guilty men,
And slays the living soul by foulness of the flesh.   55
The body darts its arrows at its sister soul,

---

[3] Marcion was a heretic of the second century, who held that there are two Gods, one the God of the Jews and the author of evil; the other the God of the New Testament, the God of goodness who manifested himself in Jesus Christ. He rejected the Old Testament and accepted only those portions of the New Testament that reveal a good and merciful God.

The soul is tossed about within the drunken brain,
From which it draws outbursts of wild insanity
Arising from the feverish poison of the flesh.
The everlasting God it splits into two Gods   60
And dares divide the indivisible Godhead;
It perishes, slain in denying one true God,
And Cain rejoices in the death of brother soul.

Where does your madness lead you, faithless Cain,
Divider blasphemous of God? Do eyes,
Befogged, the one Creater not behold?
The bleary eye in two directions turns
And ever tricks the sight with double shapes.   5
Duped by the twofold nature of the world,
You fancy that two Gods in heaven reign.
The sordid world unites the different realms
Of good and bad, but heaven obeys one Lord.
The heavenly kingdom does not have two kings   10
Because two powers control the minds of men.
The earthly man such dualism sees
And thinks two Godheads rule the separate spheres.
When he assumes that one God evil made
And one the good created, he implies   15
That these two Gods are sovereign though unlike.
How can two natures stand or reign for long,
Removed by different source from highest power
And weakened by alternate primacies?
Either there is one God with sovereign power,[4]   20
Or else, if two, each is reduced in might.
No sovereignty exists except in one
With plenitude of power, for when two claim
The primacy, each cannot have full sway.
Shared rule is never absolute, for both   25
Have not like power; the cleavage weakens might.

---

[4] Cf. Vergil, *Aeneid* 10.100.

We own one undivided, perfect God,
In whom is Christ, all perfect too and one
Who lives and ever lived above all things,[5]
And who shall live with none to share His throne.   30
The Father is all-powerful, Lord of all,
The God of hosts, Creator of the world,
The Source of being, Cause of every birth,
From whom all flows, all light and times and years
And number, who after one the second gave,   35
For number starts with one, and one alone
Cannot be counted. Since no second God
And Father is, and second Christ is not,
God prior to number is who has one Son.

He is true God, for He is first and one,   40
First in Himself and Him whom He begot.
For what does simple generation mean?
The Father and the Son by Him begot
Ere time and number, ever will be one.
Who would dare name as two the eternal One,   45
Who self-existing reigns in majesty,
And shatter thus the power of one Godhead.
Did the Father take to Himself a Son
So that one alien to Him might make two
And usher in a twofold Deity?   50
The image of the Father,[6] He is true Son,
And this same likeness proves that God is one.
No alien love or pledge unites the two,
But true affection and the essence sole,
Which God is, shapes a perfect unity.   55

This faith offends you, Marcion, this your sect
Condemns, dividing heaven between two lords.
What mists obstruct your view, what sleep benumbs

---
5 Cf. Eph. 1.21; Phil. 2.9.
6 Cf. Heb. 1.3.

Your senses, that you see two phantom forms
Disparted in a twofold heavenly realm.　　　　　　　60
If crass stupidity besets your mind,
Behold the elements clear to earthly eyes,
Signs that reveal the mystery of God.
The Father foreknew this heresy of one
Who would the Lord of light and earth divide,　　　65
And make Him twofold king of a sundered realm.
Wherefore He set before our eyes a sign
And visible proof, lest man should think two Gods
[Rule over cosmic space in diverse forms.]⁷
One fire in heaven's mighty vault gives rise　　　　70
To passing days, one sun begets the year;
Threefold, without division, in three ways
It shows its power: it shines, revolves, and burns,
It moves, it warms with heat, and gleams with light.
Here three things coexist, light, warmth, and speed,　75
Yet one same heavenly orb effects them all,
In one round faithful to its varied tasks,
And one same substance functions in all three.

Nought would I dare make equal unto God,
Nor to the Lord compare His thrall, the sun,　　　　80
But from small things the Father has decreed
That men should glimpse His might invisible.
In the glass of little things, we see things veiled
And through the known can seek the hidden truth.
No man has seen two suns unless half-blind,　　　　85
Or, if the shining sky is overcast,
When a dark cloud obstructs the brilliant rays
And breaks the mirrored fire into false orbs.
Souls have their clouds, their heavy fog;
A cataract the mind's eye veils with mist,　　　　　90
So that it cannot pierce the limpid sky
And grasp God's unity with quick insight;

---
⁷ Bergman brackets this line which appears in one MS.

The unsound gaze forms for itself two suns
And builds twin thrones for two supreme Godheads.
If two, then why not many thousand Gods,[8]   95
Why is the Deity content with two?
Was it not better to unloose whole swarms
Of deities upon the nations everywhere
And fill the world with monstrous demigods
To whom rude savages vain worship pay?   100
If different Gods a sundered heaven rule,
Then it is proper to assign to clouds,
To springs and roaring sea, to woods and hills,
Caves, rivers, winds, to furnaces and mines,
Their own divinities, each with due rights.   105

If you disdain to worship pagan gods
And would have two of equal sovereignty,
Tell me which has dominion over earth,
Which rules the stormy sea with ageless law.
Describe the realms assigned to these joint lords.   110
'One dwells,' you say, 'in his grim citadel,
Author of sin and crime, severe, unjust;
All mischief seething in the world he sowed,
And in snakes' venom soaking his new seeds,[9]
He drew creation from the fuel of death.   115
Creator of the world, he made the earth,
The sea and stars,[10] man with his frame of clay,
Which fever would consume and sin defile,
Which foul corruption of the grave would spoil.
But proper to the other is a love   120
Of holiness[11] and will to save mankind.
Two Testaments from these two sovereigns flowed:
The loving gave the New, the harsh, the Old.'
This, Marcion, is your factious reasoning,

---
8 Cf. Tertullian, *Adversus Marcionem* 1.5.
9 Cf. Vergil, *Georgics* 1.193.
10 Cf. Vergil, *Aeneid* 12.197.
11 Cf. Claudian, *Carmina Minora* 31.48.

Or frenzy rather of a mind deranged.[12] 125
We know the father of sin exists, but know
He is no God, nay even the slave of hell
Deserving sentence to the Stygian fires,
The God of Marcion, bitter, cruel, and false,
His lofty snake-crowned head begirt with clouds[13] 130
And wreathed with smoke and fire, while jealousy
That cannot bear the joys of the just
Fills his malicious eyes[14] with burning gall.
A heavy mane of writhing snakes conceals
His shoulders,[15] and the vipers lick his face.[16] 135
He draws into a knot the rebounding noose
In the slippery cord and with adroitness ties
The twisted snares, making the shackles fast.
To him belongs the art of hunting game,
Of snaring reckless creatures in his nets 140
And laying traps for prey in hidden spots.
He is a hunter grim, who ceases not
To wreak destruction on unwary souls,
A Nebroth,[17] who goes round the world, made rough
With deep ravines[18] and wooded crags, and strives 145
To waylay some by fraud and secret wiles,
To vanquish others by his giant arms
And spread his deadly triumphs far and wide.
Cold death, to what do you not drive men's hearts?[19]
Man, shame to say, disowning the Lord of life,[20] 150
Adores the cause of his ruin, the bloody fiend,
And worships the blade about to murder him!
So sweet is death to wretches charmed by sin,

---
12 Cf. Juvenal, *Satires* 14.136.
13 Cf. Vergil, *Aeneid* 4.248-249.
14 Cf. Claudian, *In Rufinum* 1.138.
15 Cf. *ibid.* 1.42.
16 Cf. *ibid.* 1.96.
17 Cf. Gen. 10.8,9.
18 Cf. Claudian, *Probino et Olybrio* 105.
19 Cf. Vergil, *Aeneid* 4.412.
20 Cf. Acts 3.14,15.

Such pleasure evil gives to darkened souls.
He of whom sin was born is deemed a god, 155
Who good with evil stained and white with black![21]
Mad equally were those who, people say,
Fever and Scurf adored in sacred fanes.

The author of iniquity is not God.[22]
In mind of fallen angel sin was bred, 160
Of one that like a mighty star once shone[23]
And with created splendor brightly burned.
All things created are from nothing made;
Not so is God, true Wisdom, and Holy Spirit,
The living Trinity that ever was, 165
But even angel ministers He made.
One from their number, fair of countenance,
Fierce in his might and by his strength puffed up,
Upraised himself with overweening pride[24]
And of his brightness made a bold display, 170
Till he persuaded some he was begot
Of his own power, and being from himself
Had drawn, to no creator owing birth.
Hence, his allies resolved to found a sect
Which holds that Satan out of darkness shone, 175
Who had, concealed by everlasting night,
Forever lived and reigned in a hidden world.
Jealous, they tell, he of a sudden thrust
His head out of the dark to ruin God's works.
But this our reason spurns, for that one faith 180
By Scripture handed down we may not doubt.
'Nought without God was made' we read; all things
By Him were made, and none not made by Him.[25]
But one that was created good and born

---
21 Cf. Juvenal 3.30.
22 Cf. Claudian, *De tertio cons. Hon.* 102.
23 Cf. Isa. 14.12.
24 Cf. Isa. 14.13,14.
25 Cf. John 1.3; Col. 1.16.

To do no wrong, pure from his origin, 185
Soon of his own free will became corrupt,
Defiled by envy and goaded by her stings.[26]
The spark of hate was fanned by jealousy,
And sudden ire inflamed his wicked heart.
He had seen how a form of clay grew warm 190
At the breath of God, and lord of earth was made,[27]
So that the land and sea and sky had learned
To shed their riches on their servant man
And yield their plenty to an earthly king.
The beast waxed proud, hate swelling in his soul, 195
And from his sullen heart drew bitter strength;
That beast, of old not prone, for wisdom kept[28]
His youthful form upright, now suddenly
Makes strange contortions with his sinuous breast[29]
And twists his shining belly in tangled coils. 200
His tongue, once single, darts his crafty speech,
And, cleft by guile, gives forth his three-forked words;[30]
From him sin took its rise, from him the fount
Of evil flowed, for he first sinned himself
And without teacher led mankind to sin. 205

The world shares in the downfall of its head,
And all the furniture of earth is marred.
As when a brigand who sets out to rob
The heedless traveler thinks not at first
Of spoil, but strikes the man opposing him, 210
That he may strip his victim of his cloak
And take the riches from his lifeless form,
So did the house of man, the bounteous earth,

---
26 Cf. Vergil, *Aeneid* 11.337.
27 After this line one MS has the verse: *qui cunctum regeret proprio moderamine mundum,* which may be translated, 'Who would with his own power rule the world.' It also appears in three other MS after lines 194 and 196.
28 Cf. Gen. 3.1.
29 Cf. Gen. 3.14.
30 Cf. Vergil, *Georgics* 3.439.

Fall into ruin when its master sinned,
Absorbing evil from its lord's misdeed. 215
Then from the sterile soil the grudging earth
Bore tares and paltry burs in tainted fields[31]
And ruined the growing wheat with barren oats.
Then having killed the shepherd, lions fierce
Learned on the blood of harmless calves to feed[32] 220
And mangle bullocks broken to the yoke.
Aroused by plaintive bleats, the rabid wolf
Forced entrance into full sheepfolds at night.
All creatures in the art of theft were skilled,
And cunning sharpened senses that were warped. 225
Although a wall the thriving gardens bound,
And vineyards with thick hedges be enclosed,
The locusts will devour the budding shoots,
And savage birds will pluck and tear the grapes.
Why speak of plants imbued with poisonous drugs 230
From which there oozed a dread death-dealing sap?
Now noxious fluid wells in tender shrubs,
Though nature once bore hemlock with no bane,
And dewy flowers that bedeck the laurel green
Gave harmless nourishment to wanton goats.[33] 235
The very elements exceed the bounds
Imposed by law and overrun all things,
Shaking the universe with riotous strength.
The battling winds lay waste the shady groves,
And forests crash, uprooted by the storms. 240
Elsewhere a raging torrent overleaps
Its banks, the limits that were set for it,
And spreading far, holds sway in ravaged fields.[34]
Yet the Creator no such fury willed
For these at birth, but the world's licentiousness, 245
Breaking through bounds, upset its peaceful laws.

---

31 Cf. Gen. 3.18; Vergil, *Eclogues* 5.37.
32 Cf. Claudian, *De cons. Stil.* 2.14.
33 Cf. Vergil, *Eclogues* 2.64.
34 Cf. Horace, *Odes* 1.2.13-20.

No wonder that the shattered elements
Are tossed about, that earth's defective frame
Is out of gear, and plagues exhaust the land.[35]
Man's conduct shows the way of sin to all,　　　　　250
Man's conduct full of folly and deceit,
Whence wars flare up, whence wanton pleasure flows,
Whence lust grows hot with murky flame, and greed
Gulps down its monstrous throat huge piles of gold,
Its thirst for riches never satisfied,　　　　　255
For avarice is increased with mounting wealth.
Hunger for gold grows keen from gain of gold.
Thence springs a crop of sins, sole root of vice,[36]
When luxury, seducer of modesty,
Sifts all the gushing springs and secret mines,　　　　　260
When empty show probes nature's mysteries
And prys into the dusty veins of earth
In hope of finding in its pitted depths
Some precious stones. For woman, not content
With native charms, affects a beauty false,　　　　　265
As if the hand of God gave her a face,
Not yet complete, that she must needs adorn
With crown of amethysts around her brow,
Or string of gems encircling her fair neck
And heavy emeralds hanging from her ears,　　　　　270
With pearls from shellfish in her hair entwined
And bands of gold securing braided locks.
It would disgust to tell the impious pains
That women take to paint the features dowered
With gifts of God, so that the skin, deprived　　　　　275
Of nature's hue, cannot be recognized.
Such is the conduct of the weaker sex,
Whose feeble mind sways with the tide of sin.[37]

---

35 Cf. Claudian, *In Rufinum* 1.370.
36 Cf. 1 Tim. 6.10.
37 Cf. Vergil, *Aeneid* 4.532.

But does not man, the woman's head and lord,
Who rules the portion torn from his own flesh,[38]   280
Who holds the weaker vessel in his power,[39]
Yield to excess? One sees old men grow soft
From luxury, though the Creator made
Their members harsh and strong with rigid bones;
It shames them to be men; they seek vain toys   285
To make them shine and lose their native strength.
They take delight in wearing flowing robes,
Not made of wool, but spoils from eastern trees,[40]
And clothe their rugged frames in checkered stuffs.[41]
They call on art to weave complex designs   290
With threads of fibers dyed in plant extracts.
The wool of beasts soft to the touch is combed.
You see one running after tunics rare
And weaving broidered robes with novel yarns
From many-colored birds, one shame to say   295
Exhaling womanlike outlandish scents
From aromatic paints and powders strange.

Indulgence rules the organs of our life,
Which the Creator in fine senses set.
For ears and eyes, for nostrils, palate, too,   300
We seek enjoyment stained with sinful arts;
And even touch, which quickens all our frame,[42]
Strives for the sweet caress of luxuries.
O sorrow! Nature's noble laws succumb,
And all her gifts submit to pleasure's reign.   305
All senses are misused, while men divert
To opposite ends[43] what God gave for their weal.
Have eyes, I ask, been placed beneath soft lids

---

[38] Cf. Gen. 2.21,22.
[39] Cf. 1 Peter 3.7.
[40] The reference is probably to silk. Cf. Vergil, *Georgics* 2.121; also Pliny, *Naturalis historia* 6.54; 11.76-77.
[41] Cf. Juvenal 2.97; also Pliny 8.196.
[42] Cf. Lactantius, *Div. inst.* 6.23.1 (Vol. 49, this series).
[43] Cf. Vergil, *Aeneid* 2.39.

That we may watch a dancer's shameful limbs
Whirl in the theatre[44] and thus pollute   310
Our wretched vision with obscene delights?
Do we draw breath and from the middle brain
Through our two nostrils send it forth again,
That with licentious pleasure we may sniff
The fragrance of a harlot's perfumed hair?   315
Did God give open ears and bid the sound
Pass through their channeled ways, that we might hear
A lute-girl's empty melodies, the twang
Of strings and banquet song of flaming lust?
Does sense of taste implanted in the mouth   320
Exist to whet the glutton's appetite
And please his palate with high-flavored meats,
That far into the night he may prolong
His feasts and tax his stomach with excess?
God has willed that by handling we should know,   325
Through sense of touch, what things are hard or soft,
What things are smooth or rough, what hot or cold;
But we our bodies pamper on soft beds
With downy comforts and fine linen spread.

Blest is the man who can with temperance use   330
The gifts bestowed, and in enjoying them
A sober limit keep, whom worldly pomp,
With its delights and wealth of tinsel show,
Does not enamor like a foolish child,
Who underneath deceptive sweetness sees   335
The hidden poison that appears as good.
Yet good and holy this once was for us,
When at creation's dawn Christ made the world.
For God saw it was good, as Moses proves,
Who of the world's beginnings was the scribe.   340
'God saw,' he says, 'that all He made was good.'[45]

---
44 Cf. Claudian, *In Eutropium* 2.359-360.
45 Cf. Gen. 1.31.

This I believe and firmly keep in mind,
Which, God inspiring him, that holy seer
Declared when he described creation's dawn:
Whatever God and Wisdom made is good.   345
The Father is the Author of all good
And with Him Christ, for Father and Son are one,[46]
Because one common nature makes them one
In will, in power, in goodness, and in love.
Yet there are not two Gods, nor makers two,   350
Since in their nature they are not distinct
Nor sundered in their works nor in their will,
But one Creator made all that was good.

No muddy stream flows from the source, no rill
Or spring is foul or turbid at its mouth,   355
But when clear waters lave the sandy banks,
They are defiled by contact with the mire.
Did horse and iron and bull and rope and oil
Have malice in them when they first were made?
When man is slain, the iron is not the cause   360
But cruel hands; and in the circus wild[47]
The horse is not the source of the mad uproar.
The mob's unreason, not the horses' speed
Runs wild; vile passion spoils a useful gift.
We know that Spartans in their wrestling bouts[48]   365
Were smeared with oil, and balm was thrall to sin;
Along a slender rope with footsteps sure
A reckless dancer mounts the lofty stage;
With flying leap the rash jump over beasts
And in the midst of mortal hazards play.   370
The bloody shows depend on public will,
And men by law are paid to risk their lives
That human members torn by blood-stained jaws

---

46 Cf. John 10.30.
47 Cf. Tertullian, *Apology* 38.4 (Vol. 10, this series).
48 Cf. Vergil, *Aeneid* 3.281.

May please a mob that takes delight in death.

To name the other follies of the world 375
Would nauseate, delights that rob mankind
Of thought of God and lead to grief and sin.
None to the highest Father lifts his mind,[49]
None sends his sighs to heaven nor regards
His Maker, mindful of his lofty birth, 380
And none directs his hope beyond the skies.
Man yields his soul to an infernal power,
Content to lie beneath his heavy load,
And groveling, gropes for fleeting earthly joys.
What earth brings forth, he sees as fair, what fame 385
Bestows, what sinful pleasure recommends,
What passes like the dust blown by the wind,
What vanishes like unsubstantial mist.
To these iniquities the powerful robber drives
Weak souls, when he invades the hearts of men 390
With his insidious powers; he sows in them
All sins and spreads his crew through every part.
There, subject to this prince, a mighty troop
Makes war and harries souls with dreadful arms:[50]
Wrath, superstition, grief, dissension, gloom, 395
Vile thirst for blood, the thirst for wine, for gold,
Ill-will, adultery, fraud, detraction, theft.[51]
Their hideous forms and threatening looks appall.
Ambition is puffed up and knowledge proud,
Eloquence rants, deceit weaves secret snares. 400
Here carping talk throughout the forum sounds,[52]
There cheap philosophy upholds the staff
Of Hercules and shows from street to street
Her naked sophists, while idolatry
Kneels at deaf altars and wax-coated stones. 405

---
49 Cf. Rom. 3.11.
50 Cf. Eph. 6.12.
51 Cf. Gal. 5.19-21; Rom. 1.29,30.
52 Cf. Ovid, *Ibid.* 232.

Alas, with what array the foe attacks
Mankind, with what armed minions does that chief
Wage war, and with what might he wins the fray!
The Chanaanite,[53] grim-helmed, springs to his aid
With close-packed troops, shaking his heavy beard   410
And brandishing his sword with mighty hand.
The Amorrhite host on the other side
With fury burns, while hordes of Gergesites
Pour over all the plain in flying ranks.
Some from a distance fight, some hand to hand.   415
On fire for battle, see the Jebusite troops;
Their golden javelins stained with dragons' blood
With deadly splendor glow and shine and slay.
It pleases you, Hethite, to arm with spears
Your dreadful bands; but Pherezites, alike   420
In spirit though not in arms, with arrows charge.
And last the Hevite king brings up his force,
His scaly breastplate made of serpent's skin.
Abetted by these troops, the wicked fiend
Subdues weak souls, who guileless and unskilled   425
In war, at first as allies trust these bands[54]
By virtue of pretended amity,
And follow Mammon through their love of peace.
Then carried off in chains, they bend their necks
Beneath a cruel yoke, and vile behests   430
Of wretched spirits they willingly obey.
One who would swell his dower with needless lands,
And scorning bounds, desires his neighbor's farm,[55]
Is being led before triumphal cars,
Hands tied behind his back and girt with chains,[56]   435
Yet knows not he is thrall to savage power.
Another scaling heights of windy fame,
Puffed up with popular applause,

---

[53] Cf. Gen. 10.15,16; Jos. 11.3; 24.11.
[54] Cf. Vergil, *Aeneid* 2.371.
[55] Cf. Horace, *Satires* 2.6.8,9.
[56] Cf. Vergil, *Aeneid* 2.57.

Deems it the greatest good to win high place,
To awe the trembling prisoner at the bar, 440
To punish wretched backs with cruel rods,
And wield the fearful axes of the law:
This man has thrust his head into the noose,
And shackled feet are chafed by slavery's chains.

Believe, O captive mortals, now condemned 445
To durance in the enemy's prison house,
In galling bondage to an occult power,
This is that Babylon, that banishment
And conquest of our race by Assyria's king,[57]
Which Jeremia mourned in tearful song, 450
Dirge for a city of its people reft.
Is it not clear that souls of Jacob's seed
Taste foreign exile in the Persian realms,
Enslaved and subject to their alien laws?
There they forget their native mode of life, 455
And putting off ancestral ways, they yield
To pagan rules, adopt new speech and dress,
Defile themselves with heathen sacrifice,
And banish Sion's nurture from their hearts.
Unmindful of their fatherland, they break 460
Their sacred harps and foreign rites observe.[58]
Was it not better for their sires to bear
The rule of Memphis' court, to warm themselves
At hostile fires, beneath grim Pharao's feet,
Inured to slavish toil in clay and straw 465
And surfeited with undigested meats?[59]

Why did the Lord preserve that rebel race
With bounty undeserved and wondrous signs,
Removing from their necks the servile chains,

---
57 Cf. 4 Kings 24.14-16.
58 Cf. Dan. 3.7.
59 Cf. Exod. 16.3.

And curbing Egypt with the serpent rod?[60]   470
What did it profit them to tread the path
Through the withdrawing sea, where flooded rocks
Lay bare beneath the unfamiliar sky,
And thirsty slime grew dry in the watery deep,
If the host that was triumphant by God's power   475
And guided through the dark by pillared fire,
Has lost that fruitful vale where grapes were found;[61]
If it tills not the land where honey flows,
And rivers are imbued with snow-white milk;
If it lets Jericho by trumpets won   480
Lift up again its ancient towering walls;
If from the refluent Jordan's[62] bank it turns
And leaves the lands apportioned out by lot;
If it cannot defend the city built
With so much sweat, and towers that rise   485
Beyond the clouds; if it knows not what stone[63]
Resists the foe, the bulwark of its walls,
Which no war engine with its brazen head
Can take by storm, nor blows of iron shake?
This cornerstone is in the portal's arch,   490
Uniting all, the threshold making firm.
The man who heeds this stone set in his walls
And with a triple bulwark girds himself,
Taking his stand on a high tower, with faith
In that true rock and with escutcheon pure,   495
Will not be ravished by the Tyrian queen,
Nor Parthian dweller on the Euphrates,
Nor swarthy Indian[64] with his feathered crown.
Nay, should the Philistine make war on you
And seek with fiery giants to raze your camp.   500
You will be safe, nor will that Charon grim,

---
60 Cf. Exod. 7.10.
61 Cf. Num. 24-27.
62 Cf. Jos. 3.16.
63 Christ, whom St. Paul calls the cornerstone; cf. Eph. 3.20.
64 Cf. Vergil, *Georgics* 4.293.

The god of Marcion who rules in realms
Of darkness, drive you from your firm stronghold.
Vain are all things the sun looks down upon,
All from short-lived and crumbling matter made. 505

Unless I err, the apostle, having said
Creation was made subject to vain strife,[65]
Deplored its bondage to the wily fiend.
'He errs,' he says, 'who thinks our wrestling is
With flesh and blood, with lust and bitter gall, 510
And that the spirit sins from veins afire.
The flesh weighs not upon the soul, the world
With the ethereal spirit does not contend,
But night and day we wage a savage war
Against the spirits of darkness in the sky, 515
Who have domain in damp and cloudy air.'[66]
In truth, the space midway 'twixt heaven and earth
That holds the clouds suspended in its void
Is the dominion of the various powers
And dwelling of Belial's wicked crew. 520
It is with robbers such as these we strive,
According to the apostle's sacred words.
Let no man nature or the sting of flesh
Blame for his sin; the passions can be tamed,
Gross creature promptings can with ease be spurned, 525
And fallen flesh and blood can be subdued.
The spirit from the heights of heaven sent[67]
Is nobler far, and if it wills to curb
The lower members with relentless laws,
No power can resist its kingly rule. 530
In man, a stronger force within instills
Its bane and subtly strikes the spiritual soul.
Not swifter flies through winds the Parthian shaft[68]

---
65 Cf. Rom. 8.20-22.
66 Cf. Eph. 6.12; 2.2.
67 Cf. Vergil, *Aeneid* 12.853.
68 Cf. *ibid.* 856-859.

Whose path cannot be seen by human eye;
For swiftly flying on the wings of air, 535
It comes unseen, and no vibrating sound
Announces death's approach, before the dart
Strikes deep into the breast its poisoned wound.
But swifter and more deadly is that shaft
The ruler of the shadowy world lets fly, 540
A dart that baffles sight in its quick course
And pierces deep into the inmost heart.

The soul by nature is not dull or slow
To dodge the blow (for God has dowered it
With spiritual fire, pure, wise, etheric, calm, 545
Lively, intent, swift, agile, penetrant),
If it but humbly praise and serve its Lord
And sternly trample under foot the world,
Delighting not in baneful wealth and spoils,
Ill-gotten, of the earth, lest crushed beneath 550
Their heavy weight and thrall to alien rule,
It cannot shun the arrows of the foe.[69]

Why blame all evil of the world and men
Upon the enemy's spite, when sins arise
From our own minds and have their source, their power, 555
And very being in the fathering heart?[70]
The tempter is the author of our sins,
But only as we will can he confuse
Or trap us; we ourselves supply the lion[71]
With abundant arms; the wild beast roars in vain 560
Unless abetted by the human will.
From our own body we beget our sin,
As David, parent blessed otherwise,
Begot the guilty Absalom;[72] he was

---
[69] Cf. Eph. 6.16.
[70] Cf. Matt. 15.19.
[71] Cf. 1 Peter 5.8.
[72] Cf. 2 Kings 14-18.

The father of one patricidal son 565
Among his blameless children, one who dared,
Alas, to draw his sword against his sire
And go to war with his own flesh and blood.
Our hearts, likewise, bring forth a vile offspring,
Who soon against us turn their vicious teeth 570
And learn to live on their begetter's woes;
For they devour their parents' fertile flesh
And feed upon the death of their forbears.
But that great king and prophet, too, of God,
The root of virgin who would bear a child, 575
Had children both ill-starred and virtuous,
For Solomon's own brother, Absalom,
Brought sorrow to a just and noble house.
Not like to Solomon, we imitate,
Base Absalom, who shed his kinsman's blood. 580

If we may quote from heathen books, or cite
Examples from the naturalists, they say[73]
The viper dies in giving birth to young,
Made fruitful by her death and not by sex
Or swelling of the womb, but at the rise 585
Of female heat, she lures her doomed consort
With open mouth; he thrusts his three-tongued head
Into her jaws and then within her mouth
He eagerly implants the venomous seed.
The bride, enraptured, clasps her lover's neck 590
And breaks it with her mordant teeth, the while
She drinks the slaver of her dying spouse.
In these delights the father dies, but soon
The prisoned young the mother kill; for when
The growing bodies in their warm retreat 595
Begin to move and strike against the womb,
The mother, conscious of her guilt, bewails
The impious malice of her murderous brood

[73] Cf. Pliny, *Nat. hist.* 10.169.

As they break through the barriers to their birth.
For since no vent for giving birth exists, 600
The young lash at the belly as they strive
To reach the light through lacerated sides.
Then at the mother's death the dolorous troop
Comes forth with scarce a struggle, as they carve
Their way to life by crime; they slowly lick 605
The corpse that bore them, orphans at their birth
And posthumous children of their wretched dam.

Thus does our soul conceive: thus does it drink
The deadly venom from the serpent's mouth,
Wed to Belial's son; thus it admits 610
His vile embrace, thus it is filled with sins,
United with a partner doomed to die.
Then it conceives and spawns a lethal brood
Of vicious works from seed of that vile snake,
Which by its pains must pay the penalty 615
For ravishing the soul and all the world.
Cruel wounds torment the soul, the thousand pains
Of childbirth, as her monstrous progeny
She brings to life, a multitude of sins,
Offspring that on their mother's corpse have fed. 620

Hence comes that harsh reproach of Christ the Lord:
'Is not the devil, ye unjust, I charge,
The father who begot you in the flesh,
Desirous of iniquity?'[74] Peruse
The holy book: the Lord in words like these 625
Rebuked unholy men: 'For love,' He says,
'And acts of love would prove you to be sons
Of my Father.'[75] O sightless lust! How can
The soul that knows herself to nuptials true
Affianced, called to marriage with a king, 630

---
[74] Cf. John 8.44.
[75] Cf. John 8.41,42.

One always young and never growing old,
With countenance of lasting charm divine,
Choose vile adultery and sell herself
To foul embraces of the prince of night,
Spurning the Son of God of Virgin born   635
And deeming children of a brothel sweet?

I know the crafty charge against us hurled,
With what sharp tooth relentless malice fights,
And by attacking truth, calls us to strife.
'If God wills not that evil be,' it says,   640
'Why does He not forbid it? Whether He
Created it or lets his fairest works
Be spoiled by sin, means naught, when He has power
To hinder it; if the Almighty willed
All to live pure, no deed the will or hand   645
Would stain. Therefore, the Lord created sin,
Which He beholds from heaven and tolerates
As though He made it; for He has himself
Made all He sanctions or allows to be.'

Stop up my ears, good Father, close   650
The winding channels of my foolish head,
Lest it drink in such sounds; great gain it is
To lose one vital function of the brain
If, owing to a deafened ear, the soul
May be kept free from hearing blasphemy.   655
Who mindful of his excellence, derived
From heavenly gifts, would bear these vile affronts
Against his God? In brief, God's love is proved
When fallen man He raises from the tomb
And His celestial kingdom bids him share   660
For all eternity. If He were cause
And stay of evil, He would not have willed
To save the sinner by redeeming grace
When he incurred salvation's loss and death.

It is of man to fall, of God to save: 665
Man dies because of sin, which God blots out,
Proof that He wills not evil, nor approves
Beforehand what He afterwards forgives.

'Can any sin despite the Thunderer's will,
The will of Him who has the power to sway 670
The heart of man, to foster chaste desires,
And in his bosom every virtue plant?'
Do you not know, O fool, the liberty
Your Maker gave you? Know you not what power
Was at Creation granted you to rule 675
The subject earth and your own spirit, the power
Of free will, right to will and do all things
As you see fit, with free untrammeled soul?
When He made you the lord of all the earth
And bade Creation bow to your commands, 680
Gave land, sky, sea, streams, winds for your domain,
Would He have grudgingly withheld free will
And liberty denied as not your due?
How strong would be the chosen lord of earth[76]
If he were not the ruler of himself? 685
How lordly one whose spirit is not free,
But subject to a stern unwavering law?
What praise for virtue does a man deserve
Unless he must make choice between two paths?
He does good freely only when the power 690
Is his to will and choose the opposite.
He is not good, nor does he merit praise
Who is not virtuous of his own free will,
For virtue is ignoble that is forced;
And virtue there is none unless it springs 695
From spurning wrong and seeking righteousness.

'Go,' Adam's Father, God, and Maker says,

---
[76] Cf. Gen. 1.28.

'Go forth, O Man, exalted by my breath,[77]
Not subject made, great ruler of the world
And ruler of your own free spirit, to me   700
Alone be subject with a bondage free.
I bind you not by force, but counsel you
To flee injustice and the right pursue.
Light is to virtue joined, and death to vice.
Choose life![78] Uprightness leads to lasting bliss,   705
And sin, in turn, will bring eternal doom;
You have the freedom to decide your lot.'
Made sovereign by this love and bounteous gift
Man scorns these precepts, freely choosing death,
And deems more useful what the crafty snake   710
Prompts him to do against the will of God.[79]
The fiend prevailed by urging, not by force;
The woman answered when rebuked by God
That she by sly persuasion had been won,[80]
Then urged the man, who freely followed her.   715
Was he not free to spurn her tempting words
With upright soul? He was, for God before
Had warned him to do good of his own will,
But minding not, he yielded to the foe.
Between the Lord of life and lord of death   720
He stands: God calls him here, the devil there,
And dubious, he shifts from side to side.

Hear now a famous record of events
Wherein the Scriptures traced a moral clear.
From burning Sodom, Lot was hurrying forth[81]   725
And leading with him all his dear household
To save them from the blazing town; the air

---
77 Cf. Gen. 2.7.
78 Cf. Deut. 30.19; Sir. (Ecclus.) 15.14-18.
79 Cf. Gen. 3.1-6.
80 Cf. Gen. 3.13.
81 Cf. Gen. 19.23.

Was filled with sulphurous clouds that veiled the sun,[82]
And rattling brimstone set the sky afire.
An angel sent by God in twofold form[83]   730
Had given orders that the family
Should leave the city gates, and with their eyes
Fixed on the plain, should not turn back to look
Upon the fires that raged within the walls.
'Let none, once he has stepped outside the gate,   735
Of Sodom think, the type of earth's downfall,
Nor turn his head to gaze upon the ruins.'
Lot listened to this warning, but his wife,
A fickle woman, backwards turned her glance
And clung to her dear Sodom's luring charms.   740
Eve had enticed her lord to share her sin,
But Lot's wife only perished for her fault:
Her body turned to frail dissolving stone,
She stands a woman as she stood before,
A pillar of salt that all her likeness keeps,   745
Her grace, her dress, her brow, her eyes, and hair,
Her face turned backwards and her chin inclined,
The stark memorial of an ancient sin.[84]
Her moist form dissolves in salty sweats,
But is not lessened by the dripping waste;   750
However much the cattle lick away
Enough is left of moisture, and the skin
That has been worn away is soon restored.
This monument the sinning wife deserved,
Who let her wavering spirit melt away   755
In lax resolves and flouted heaven's commands.
But Lot pressed on with resolution firm,
Nor did he turn to view the town reduced
To ashes like a mighty funeral pyre,
Its people and their life destroyed, its scrolls,   760

---
82 Cf. Vergil, *Aeneid* 3.582.
83 Cf. Gen. 19.1.
84 Cf. Josephus, *Jewish Antiquities* 1.204.

Its laws and forums, shops, resorts of vice,
Its temples, theatres, circus, flowing bars.
The fires of Sodom all the deeds of men
Devour in righteous flames, by Christ's decree.
It is enough to have escaped these once; 765
Our Lot does not look back, but his frail wife
Turns round to view the town from which she fled
And in its embers now stands petrified.

Behold herein a sign of our free will,
By which God wished to make us understand 770
The path we tread depends on us alone,
And we are free to follow either way.
Two were enjoined to flee from Sodom's walls:
One goes with haste, the other hesitates;[85]
Each has free will, but each diversely wills. 775
Each by his choice is drawn in opposite ways.
Examples can be found in Holy Writ:
Mark Ruth and Orpha of the Moab race![86]
One follows Noemi with trusting love,
The other leaves her. Then no longer bound 780
By wedlock and the Hebrew marriage rites,
They now were free, but Orpha's ancient faith
Led her to choose a Gentile mate and rear
The stock from which the fierce Goliath sprang.
Ruth, gleaning in the sunny fields, the hand[87] 785
Of Boaz won, and in a wedlock chaste
Brought forth the race of Christ, king David's line,[88]
And linked her mortal progeny with God.[89]

I call to mind how often brothers twain
Have reached a crossroad and reflected long. 790

---
85 Cf. Vergil, *Aeneid* 4.641.
86 Cf. Ruth 1.4.
87 Cf. Ruth 2.3.
88 Cf. Ruth 4.17-22.
89 Cf. Matt. 1.5-16.

Uncertain what the better way might be,
For on the right a thorny wood hemmed in
The narrow trail, and up along a cliff
A rocky footpath led to airy heights,
While on the left a shady grove stretched fair[90]   795
Through grassy meadows, rich with luscious fruits,
Where ran a gently sloping road. One chose
To creep through briers up the lofty crags,
The other took the plain upon the left;
One thrust his head into the nearby stars,   800
The other fell into a miry swamp.
All have like nature but do not attain
Like ends, for their resolves take different forms.
At times it chances that a flock of doves,
All milky white, fly down from cloudless heights   805
Into a field where fowlers' traps are laid,
Twigs smeared with sticky lime and snares bestrewn
With peas or treacherous meal: some are deceived
By tempting grains and tangle avid beaks
In chains of twisted hair, or glue restrains   810
Their fettered wings, but others not allured
By love of eating, walk about unharmed
Upon the barren grass and take good care
To keep their eyes turned from the artful bait.
When time comes for returning to the sky,   815
Some freely seek the heavens and clap their wings
High in the air, while others captive lie
And wounded, scan the breezy heights in vain.

So nature pours on earth from heavenly founts
Souls of one color, but seductions sweet   820
There hold them fast, and few ascend again
To heaven, while many feast on viscous food
And cannot rise to higher realms above.

---
90 Cf. Vergil, *Aeneid* 6.473; 638.

Therefore, the Father kindled Tartarus,
Made black with molten lead, and trenches dug   825
In dark Avernus for the streams of hell,
And in the gulf of Phlegethon bade worms
To dwell for sin's eternal punishment.[91]
He knew that to our frame His breath gave life,
And that the soul formed by the eternal lips   830
Could never die, nor when once stained with sin,
Could it return to heaven, but must be plunged
Into the burning depths of hell's abyss.
To worms and flames and tortures lasting time
He gave, so that the sufferings might not cease   835
For the undying soul: torments consume
And keep alive the substance without end,
While death compels the groaning wretch to live.
But far away in realms of paradise
The Majesty divine has planned rewards   840
For spirits pure and free from every stain
That have not on Gomorrha's ruins looked back,
But with averted gaze have left behind
The wicked world now hastening to its doom.
First they are borne with easy flight to heaven   845
Whence Adam's soul at his creation flowed;
For since the stress of life cannot hold back
Its subtle nature, nor impede its course,
The glowing spirit cleaves the heavy air
And leaves the sky behind in its disdain   850
Of earth, the prison house of its exile.
Then when the soul attains its heavenly home
Faith takes her to her bosom and consoles
Her foster child, who tells in plaintive words
The labors of her sojourn in the flesh.   855
There, lying on a purple couch, she breathes
The perfumes of eternal flowers and drinks

---

[91] Cf. Mark 9.43.

Ambrosial dew from roses, while she spurns
The rich men thirsting in the distant flames
For streams and showers of heaven, and begging her   860
To put her dewy finger in their mouths
And quench the fiery darts with its moist touch.[92]

You should not wonder that, though far apart,
Souls damned and just each other clearly see
And note the portion each has merited,   865
Across the space that heaven and hell divides.
He errs who would ascribe to souls the sight
Of human eyes, which in a glassy film
Are shrouded, and in which a misty fluid
A mirror forms that blocks their faltering view.   870
Do round drops from the eyes of souls gush forth,
Or are they veiled by lashes thick and rough
And covered by a screen of shading lids?
Their sight is keen, their pupil is a fire
That pierces clouds and darkness penetrates.   875
No substance black or solid blocks their gaze,
The murky clouds of night give way to them,
Before them lies the whole round universe.
Not only does the soul with vision keen
Traverse the air, but through the mountains high   880
To ocean's end and Thule's farthest shores[93]
It passes, and to hell it sends its glance.
All colors night blots out for human eyes
And in the darkness every shape is lost.
Do those who have put off their fleshly frames   885
Lose power of seeing, or mistake their way?
One shape, one hue of air encloses souls,
On right or left, as is the due of each.[94]
The change of time does not reverse their lot,

---

92 Cf. Luke 16.19-26.
93 Cf. Vergil, *Aeneid* 4.480; *Georgics* 1.30; Seneca, *Medea* 379.
94 Cf. Matt. 25.31-41.

Which lasts always, whatever it may be.[95] 890
Through all the ages one same course revolves.
Can there be doubt that souls see things concealed
From bodily eyes, when often in our sleep
The spirit beholds vast regions far away
And darts its glance through fields and stars and seas? 895
For not before our death does it depart
From living members, nor resign its home
Of flesh and blood, withdrawing from the heart
And robbing it of life, but while it stays
Within its carnal house, it probes all things 900
With piercing eyes, directing far the gaze
Of its ethereal nature no material thing
Obstructs, and views the world before it spread,
With black abysses down below the earth.
The ground between does not impede its sight. 905
If it should turn its face to stars above,
Naught in between would block the fiery gaze
Of the unsleeping soul, though heavy clouds
And veil of darkness cover all the sky.
Thus John sees secrets in the future hid[96] 910
While in the body still and bound by flesh,
But freed by grace of sleep from carnal ties,
He wanders for awhile with piercing eyes
Through scenes ordained for years and days to come.
He sees the angels armed in readiness 915
For the destruction of the world by fire,
And hears the trumpets sounding at its end.[97]
He saw all this with soul withdrawn awhile,
But not yet from the body loosed in death.
Will not the spirit more clearly see all things 920
When in the grave its mortal vesture lies?
We hold that fires of that infernal night

---
95 Cf. Vergil, *Aeneid* 9.164; 2.49.
96 Cf. Apoc. 1.9,10.
97 Cf. Apoc. 8.6,7.

In which souls stained by sin forever burn[98]
The poor man sees from his far-off abode;[99]
Likewise, the golden crowns won by the just   925
Are shown across the intervening gulf
To souls confined in hell's dread prison house.
His ulcers healed, the soul in paradise
Beholds the torments of the reprobate,[100]
And each has knowledge of the other's need.   930

O God the Father, Author of our soul,
O Christ, God from whose mouth the Spirit proceeds,
One God, Thy law directs and guides my life,
Thy judgment makes me tremble and grow pale;
Thy judgment makes me hope for pardon, too,   935
Unworthy though I be in words and deeds.
These I confess; forgive and pardon me.
I merit punishment, but deign, good Judge,
To cancel what is due and freely grant
A better lot in answer to my prayers.   940
When my poor soul has quit this mortal frame
Made up of sinews, skin, blood, gall, and bones,
To which, alas, its pampered inmate clings,
When death has closed these eyes, and cold I lie,
When vision clear my naked spirit enjoys,   945
Let it not see one of those demons fierce,
Relentless, grim, with threatening look and voice,
Prepared to drag me, stained with many sins,
Headlong into black yawning caves below,
There to exact from me all that is due,   950
To the last farthing, for my wasted life.[101]
Thy Father's house has mansions manifold,[102]
O Christ. I do not ask Thee for a home

---
98 Cf. Matt. 13.42.
99 Cf. Luke 16.26.
100 Cf. Luke 16.19-26.
101 Cf. Matt. 5.26.
102 Cf. John 14.2.

In regions of the blest; let those chaste throngs
Dwell there, who scorning things of earth, have sought   955
Thy riches, and the virgins innocent,
Who have renounced all carnal appetites.[103]
Enough that I behold no slave of hell,
And that Gehenna's flames may not devour
My soul in its abysmal furnace plunged.   960
Let fire of deep Avernus swallow me,
Since only thus may carnal stain be cleansed,
But let the smoldering flames breathe gentle heat,
And let their ardor languish and grow cool.
To others be eternal light and crowns,   965
To me be penance swift and merciful.

---

[103] Cf. Matt. 19.12.

THE SPIRITUAL COMBAT

(PSYCHOMACHIA)

THE SPIRITUAL COMBAT

Preface

Of true believers first, that faithful patriarch,[1]
Abram, of blessed seed in waning years the sire,
Whose name was lengthened by an added syllable,
Called Abram by his father, Abraham by God,[2]
Who gave in sacrifice the child born past his prime,   5
Thus teaching us, with lively faith in God,
To place upon the altar as a pious gift
The dearest and the only treasure of our heart,
Has counseled us to fight against unholy tribes,
By his example urging us and showing us   10
That we beget no offspring worthy in God's sight,
With Virtue as a mother, till the militant soul,
In battle fierce, has overcome with many blows
The evil monsters reigning in our captive heart.

One day ferocious kings made Lot their prisoner,[3]   15
When he in wicked Sodom and Gomorrha dwelt,
The cities that he loved, where though a foreigner,
He had great power by reason of his uncle's fame.
Aroused by heralds of misfortune, Abram hears
His kinsman, taken prisoner in a luckless war,   20
Is held in bondage by his alien conquerors.
Three hundred and eighteen domestic slaves he arms[4]
In quick pursuit against the fleeing enemy,

---
1 Cf. Gen. 15.6; Gal. 3.6-9.
2 Cf. Gen. 17.5.
3 Cf. Gen. 14.12.
4 Cf. Gen. 14.14.

Encumbered by the treasures and abundant spoils
That have been taken in their glorious victory.   25
He, too, unsheathes his sword, inspired by love of God,
And puts to flight the haughty kings, weighed down by spoils,
Or mows them down and tramples them beneath his feet.
He breaks the captives' chains and rescues stolen goods:
The gold, the maidens, children, jeweled necklaces,   30
The droves of mares, the urns, the robes, the heifer calves.[5]
Lot, set at liberty by loosing of his chains,
Unbends his neck delivered from the galling links.
The haughty foe now scattered, Abraham returns
In triumph, bringing back with him his brother's son,   35
That evil kings might not in cruel slavery hold
The scion of a family of faithful blood.
To that heroic chief, fresh from the battlefield,
The priest presents the holy bread from heaven above,[6]
The priest of God, likewise a king of might and power   40
Whose mystic origin from source ineffable
No author in the sacred scriptures has made known,[7]
Melchisedech, whose race and ancestry lie hid[8]
And are not understood except by God alone.
Then in the form of three angelic visitors[9]   45
God at the entrance of the old man's tent appears,
While Sara is amazed to feel her youth renewed,
As in her womb she past the usual time conceives,
And gladdened by an heir, her former laughter rues.[10]

This preface has been given here to symbolize   50
The likeness that our life should faithfully portray:

---

5 In Bergman this line reads: *oves, equarum vasa, vestem, buculas,* after one MS. All the others have *greges* instead of *oves;* cf. note in Lavarenne's edition, page 69.
6 Cf. Gen. 14.18.
7 Bergman regards lines 41 and 42 as interpolations and brackets them in his text.
8 Cf. Heb. 7.3.
9 Cf. Gen. 18.1.
10 Cf. Gen. 18.10-14.

Clad in the armor of true hearts,[11] we must keep watch,
And every portion of our body, which is held
In durance and enslaved to shameful appetites,
Must be set free by mustering all our inner strength, 55
For we are rich in servants born within our house,
If through the mystic symbol we discern the power
Inherent in three hundred with twice nine subjoined.[12]
Hereafter Christ himself, who is the true high priest,[13]
Born of a Father, mighty and unnamable, 60
Supplying bread from heaven to the victors blest,
Will enter the humble dwelling of the sinless heart
And cheer it with a visit from the Trinity;[14]
And then the Holy Spirit will embrace the soul,
So long denied offspring, and by a marriage chaste, 65
Will make it fruitful with the seed of heavenly grace,
And late in life, thus richly dowered, it will fill
The household of the Father with a worthy heir.

Christ, ever of man's woes compassionate,[15]
Great in the Father's power and in Thy own,
One power—for by both names one God we praise,
But not alone, since Thou, O Christ, art God,
Born of the Father—say, our King, what arms 5
The soul may wield to drive sin from the heart,
When our unruly passions rise within,
And war against the vices tires our spirit,
What tower of strength can guard our liberty,
Or battle line oppose the fiends that rage 10
Within our breast. For not without the aid

---

11 Cf. Eph. 6.11-17.
12 According to some commentators, the reference here is to the 318 bishops of the Nicene Council, who confirmed the faith and destroyed heresies. The number 318 (in Greek TIH) was also considered as a symbol of Christ, T representing the cross and IH the first two letters of the name Jesus. Cf. P.L. 59.712 ff.
13 Cf. Heb. 5.5-10; 6.20; 7.15-22.
14 An allusion to the Holy Eucharist.
15 Cf. Vergil, *Aeneid* 7.56; Paulinus of Nola, *Carmina* 18.261 (PL 61.496).

Of mighty Virtues hast Thou, gracious Lord,
Exposed to warring Vices Christian souls.
Thou sendest saving troops to fight within
The body sore beset, Thou dost array 15
The spirit with arms to battle evil thoughts,
To strive for Thee, to overcome for Thee.
The way of victory will be made clear
If we the Virtues' very forms may show
And monstrous Vices that with them contend. 20

Faith first the field of doubtful battle seeks,
In careless rustic dress, with shoulders bare,
With flowing locks and naked arms exposed;
For in her sudden zeal for new conflicts,
She takes no thought of weapons or of shield, 25
But trusting her stout heart and unclad limbs,
She risks the hazards of a savage fray.
Idolatry soon rallies all her strength
And dares to come to blows with warlike Faith.
But rising to full height,[16] Faith fells the foe, 30
With fillets crowned, and buries in the dust[17]
The mouth filled with the victim's blood; the eyes
Forced out in death,[18] she tramples under foot;
The channels of the shattered throat are blocked,
And weary gasps augment the pangs of death. 35
The host exults, a thousand martyrs swift,
Which Faith, their Queen, had launched against the foe.
And now she crowns her brave allies with flowers,
And orders them with purple to be clothed.

Next on the grassy plain is Modesty 40
In gleaming armor, ready for the strife.
On comes the Sodomite, Voluptousness

---

[16] Cf. Vergil, *Aeneid* 12.902.
[17] Cf. *ibid.* 12.303.
[18] Cf. *ibid.* 8.260.

With fire-brands girt, and thrusts a torch of pine
Into her face and modest eyes, intent
On blinding her with flames and pitchy smoke.[19]   45
The maid, undaunted, flings a heavy rock
Against the lustful fury's hand and torch,
And from her sacred face wards off the brand.[20]
Then with her sword the disarmed harlot's throat
She pierces through; the fiery fumes gush forth   50
With clots of blood, and fetid breath exhaled
Defiles the air in all the neighborhood.
'She has it,'[21] cries the Queen in triumph; 'This
Shall be thy end, and prostrate shalt thou lie
Forever; thou shalt never dare to hurl   55
Thy flames against God's servants, whose pure hearts
Are kindled from the torch of Christ alone.
Have you, O plague of men, your strength renewed,
Grown warm again with breath of life once quenched,
Long after Holofernes' severed head   60
Drenched his Assyrian bed with lustful blood,
And Judith, scorning his bejeweled couch
Stopped short his impure passion with the sword,
And, woman though she was, brought back the prize,
Avenging me with valor heaven-inspired.[22]   65
This woman, fighting still beneath the Law,
Had little strength, though of our age a type,[23]
When into earthly frames true power has flowed,
Through which weak hands cut off a mighty head.
Now that a Virgin has brought forth a Child,   70
Where is your power?—That virgin motherhood,
In which the natural birth of man was changed
And Power from on high the new flesh formed,[24]

---
19 Cf. *ibid.* 9.72-76; Statius, *Thebaid* 11.492-495.
20 Cf. Vergil, *Aeneid* 9.109.
21 Cf. *ibid.* 12.296.
22 Cf. Judith 13.17-25.
23 Cf. 1 Cor. 10.11.
24 Cf. Luke 1.35.

In which a Maid unwed conceived God, Christ,
Man from His Mother, but with His Father God. 75
All flesh is now divine which gave Him birth,
And by this union, in God's nature shares,[25]
The Word made flesh has never ceased to be
The everlasting Word, though joined to flesh;
His majesty by union with the flesh 80
Is not abased, but lifts up wretched men.
What He was ever, He remains, and now
Begins to be what He was not; we are
Not what we were, but born to a better state.
Gift of Himself does not His Godhead dwarf, 85
But by it we are raised to heavenly gifts.
These gifts confound you, O Voluptuousness,
Nor after Mary can you break my laws.
You lead to death, you are the door of ruin;[26]
Through body's stain, you plunge the soul in hell. 90
In that black gulf now hide your head, vile scourge;
Die, harlot; seek the dead; may you be thrust
Into the depths of hell and darkest night.
May nether streams roll you in fiery waves,
And pools of sulphur whirl you in their flood. 95
No more tempt Christian souls, O chief of fiends,[27]
That bodies, henceforth pure, may serve their King.'
Her discourse ended, Modesty rejoiced
That Voluptuousness lay dead, and in the waves
Of Jordan's stream, she washed her sword, all stained 100
With gore that had befouled the shining blade.
By that baptism in the cleansing flood
The victress purifies her conquering sword
Of bloodstain from the enemy's foul throat,
But not content to sheathe the spotless steel, 105
Lest hidden rust defile its gleaming face,

---

25 Cf. 2 Peter 1.4.
26 Cf. Lucretius 1.1112.
27 Cf. Vergil, *Aeneid* 3.252.

Upon the altar of a Catholic shrine
She offers it, to shine with fadeless light.

Lo, Patience stood with countenance serene,
Unmoved amid the strife and mad uproar, 110
And watched with steady eyes the deadly wounds
Made by the darts, as action she delayed.
From far-off Anger, foaming at the mouth,
Turns on her eyes suffused with blood and gall
And taunts her for her sloth with words and blows.[28] 115
Impatient, she lets fly a lethal pike,
Shaking the bearded plumes on her helmet's crown.[29]
'Take this,' she cries, 'dull witness of our fight,
Receive in your quiet breast this deadly steel,
And wince not, since for you to moan is shame.' 120
She speaks thus, and the shaft hurled through the air
Follows her angry words; then swerving not,
It strikes the stomach with unerring blow,
But springs aside, stopped by the hard cuirass.
For Patience had put on a coat of mail 125
No steel could pierce, a threefold fabric made[30]
Of iron scales, with leather interlaced.
She stands unruffled, facing all the darts
Upon her rained, and bears the blows unpierced.
Disturbed not by the frenzied monster's lance 130
She waits for Anger's death by her own rage.
Then when the vixen all her strength had spent
In frenzied raving, when the futile shower
Of javelins had worn out her strong right arm,
When flying missiles fell with no effect 135
And useless shafts lay broken on the ground,
She reaches for her sword, and raising it
Above her ear,[31] she hurls the shining blade

---
28 Cf. *ibid.* 10.644.
29 Cf. *ibid.* 12.493.
30 Cf. *ibid.* 3.467.
31 Cf. *ibid.* 9.417.

And strikes midway her foe's unbending head.
The brazen helmet at the blow resounds 140
And by its hardness blunts the rebounding blade;
The stubborn metal breaks the smiting steel,
As it, unyielding, meets the vain assault
And thwarts unharmed the striker's vicious thrust.
When Anger sees the fragments of her sword 145
Roll clattering afar, still holding fast
The bladeless hilt, distraught she throws away
The useless ivory, sign of her disgrace,
And flings afar the painful souvenir,
As passion urges her to end her life. 150
From missiles launched in vain, one from the dust
She then picks up for this nefarious use.
Into the ground she thrusts the polished wood
And on the upturned point she stabs herself.
Then Patience standing over her, cries out: 155
'With wonted valor we have crushed this Vice
Without endangering our blood or life;
This is our rule of war, to quell the hosts
Of evil by endurance of their blows.
Foe to itself is rage, and Anger has slain 160
Herself and dies by her own fiery darts.'
So speaking, through the battle lines unharmed
She passes with a great hero; for Job[32]
To his unconquered leader had kept close;
Grave hitherto and panting from bloodshed, 165
But smiling now at wounds and ulcers healed,
He reckons up the thousand battles won,
His own rewards, his enemy's disgrace.
The Virtue bids him rest from strife of arms,
Restore his losses with the captured spoils, 170
And bring back treasures that would never fade.
She breaks through legions dense and charging lines,

---

32 Cf. Job 1-3.

Advancing scatheless through wound-bringing showers.
To all the Virtues Patience is allied,
Their brave companion and their only aid;   175
No Virtue dares to enter combat fierce,
Unless by Patience she is fortified.

That moment, Pride was galloping about
Upon a fiery steed, on whose strong flanks
A heavy lion's skin she had arranged,   180
That proudly seated on the wild beast's mane,
She might look down upon the ranks with scorn.
High on her head her braided hair was piled,[33]
So that the mass enhanced her shining locks
And made a lofty crown above her brow.   185
A linen scarf that from her shoulders hung
Was caught into a knot upon her breast;[34]
A veil of gossamer flowed from her neck
And caught the breezes in its billowing folds.
No less vainglorious is her restless horse,   190
His mouth impatient of the curbing bit.[35]
He foams with rage and turns from side to side,
Galled at restraint and pressure of the reins.
Parading in this style, the proud upstart
Now overtops both lines and circles round   195
Upon her horse, as she with threatening look
Surveys the scant and ill-provided force
Humility had gathered for the war;
A queen, indeed, but lacking foreign aid,
She was not trustful of her own reserves.   200
As her copartner she had chosen Hope
Whose wealth is in a realm above the earth.
When maddened Pride beheld Humility,
With no display of weapons or supplies,

---
[33] Cf. Juvenal 6.502; Tertullian, *De cultu feminarum* 2.7 (Vol. 40, this series).
[34] Cf. Vergil, *Aeneid* 11.776.
[35] Cf. Ovid, *Amores* 1.2.15.

Her voice she poured forth in bitter words:[36]   205
'Does it not shame you, wretches, to attack
Illustrious leaders with plebeian troops,
To take the sword against a noble race
Whose warlike valor conquered ancient wealth
And gave it power to rule these verdant hills?   210
An alien strives to banish old-time kings!
Lo! these are they who would our sceptres take,[37]
Who seek to till our cultivated fields,
To spoil with foreign plow our captured soil
And dispossess by war a hardy folk!   215
O foolish mob! All mankind we ensnare
At birth, while limbs are from the mother warm;
We spread our power through the new born frame
And have dominion over infant bones.
What place was given you in our domain   220
When realms acquired at birth increased in strength?
For we and our dominion one same day
Were born and have grown old with equal years
Since new-created man from narrow bounds
Of paradise fled forth into the world,   225
And Adam clothed himself in skins of beasts,[38]
Nude still, had he not followed our precepts.
What foe from shores unknown now rises up
To plague us, sluggish, sad, ill-bred, inane,
Who claims her rights so late, till now exiled?   230
No doubt, the silly talk will be believed,
Which bids the wretched hope for future bliss,
That promised happiness may soothe their sloth
With idle dreams of better things to come.
Why does this hope not tempt these raw recruits,   235
Whom blare of War's fierce trumpet does not rouse,
And languid virtue makes unfit for strife?

---

36 Cf. Vergil, *Aeneid* 10.368.
37 Cf. *ibid.* 9.600.
38 Cf. Gen. 3.21.

Is Chastity's chill heart of use in war
Or Piety's kind work performed by arms?
O Mars and our known prowess, shame it is   240
For us to fight against such soldiery,
Such trifling scum, a band of dancing girls,
Where mingle Justice and poor Honesty,
Thirsty Sobriety, pale Fasting, too,
Wan Purity, her cheeks scarce tinged with blood,   245
Simplicity exposed to every wound
And prostrate on the ground, Humility,
Whose groveling fear betrays her cowardice.
Like stubble, I will trample under foot
This helpless band, for with our seasoned swords   250
We do not deign to strike them, nor to stain
Our blades in a disgraceful victory.'

Thus shouting, she now spurs her swift war horse,[39]
And dashes madly forward with loose reins,
Intent on overthrowing her mild foe   255
And trampling her dead body in the dust.
But quick she falls into a hidden pit,
Deceit had slyly dug across the field,
Deceit, one of the Vices most despised,
A cunning trickster, who foreseeing war,   260
Had cut blind trenches in the level plain
So that onrushing troops might be stopped short
And in a treacherous ditch be swallowed up.[40]
Then lest the cautious army might detect
The artful snare, she hid the banks with twigs   265
Covered with turf to look like level ground.
The humble queen stood on the other side
And, unaware, had not drawn near the pit
Nor set foot on Deceit's malignant trap.
As Pride dashed up, she fell into the snare   270

---
39 Cf. Vergil, *Aeneid* 2.679.
40 Cf. Claudian, *In Eutropium* 2.438-439.

And thus revealed the treacherous gulf below.
Thrown forward on the horse's neck, she falls
Beneath his broken legs, crushed by his weight,
But when Humility beholds her foe
Outdone and lying at the point of death, 275
She steps up calmly with her head scarce raised
And moderates her joy with a kindly glance.
At this, Hope proffers an avenging sword
And fires her with a love of rightful praise.
Grasping her adversary by the hair, 280
She draws her forth, with suppliant face upturned;
Then bending back her head, she severs it[41]
And holds it up by gory dripping locks.

Thus Hope with sacred words reproves the vice:
'Cease your grand talk! God shatters arrogance,[42] 285
The mighty fall, the braggart proud is crushed.
Learn to renounce all pride, learn to avoid
The pit before your feet, all you who boast.
Those words of Christ are true and known by all:
The humble are upraised, the proud abased.[43] 290
We have marked how Goliath, brave and strong,
Fell by a feeble hand: a boy's sling
Hurled through the air a little stone that pierced
The giant's forehead with a gaping wound.[44]
As he, defiant, stark, proud, fierce, and grim, 295
Exulted in unbridled rage and ire,
As he paraded with his frightful shield,
He learned the power of a boy's sport
And, warrior bold, he fell to youthful years.
That lad then followed me in valor's dawn, 300
And to my realm he raised his virile soul,

---
41 Cf. Vergil, *Aeneid* 10.536.
42 Cf. 1 Peter 5.5; James 4.6.
43 Cf. Matt. 23.12.
44 Cf. 1 Kings 17.4 ff.

For at the feet of God is kept for me
A sure abode, and victors freed from guilt
Seek me when summoned to celestial heights.'
She spoke, and beating the air with golden wings,[45]   305
The maiden flies to heaven. As she goes,
The Virtues, marveling, long to follow her,
But they must stay to lead in earthly wars.
The Vices they attack and wait their crowns.

From western boundaries Sensuality,   310
A foe long reckless of her name, had come,
With scented locks, slow voice, and wandering eyes;
Lost in delights, she lived to pamper flesh,
To cramp the spirit, perversely to imbibe
Seductive sweets and enervate the mind.   315
She then was belching up a night-long feast.
For lying still at table, she had heard
The trumpets sound at dawn, and leaving cups,
With step that slipped in wine and scent, she tread
On flowers, as drunken she advanced to war.   320
Yet not on foot, but in a chariot borne,
She won the hearts of her admiring foes.
O novel clash of arms! No arrow flies
From her bowstring, no hissing lance darts forth
From twisted thong, no threatening sword she wields,   325
But flings in sport rose leaves and violets
And scatters flowers on the enemy's lines.
The Virtues charmed, with her seductive breath
She breathes a poison through their weakened frames;[46]
The scent subdues their lips, their hearts, and arms,   330
And softens iron muscles robbed of strength.
Disheartened, they lay down their javelins,
Their hands now basely limp, as stupefied,
They marvel at the chariot all agleam

---
[45] Cf. Vergil, *Aeneid* 9.14; Tibullus 4.1.209.
[46] Cf. Vergil, *Georgics* 4.236; *Aeneid* 8.390.

With gems of various hues, and longing gaze 335
At tinkling gilded reins, at axle wrought
Of solid gold, and shining round of spokes
Of silver, which the wheel's encircling rim
Embraces with its orb of amber pale.
And now the whole cohort, with standards turned, 340
Was yearning to submit with willing hearts
To Sensuality, to bear the rule,
Of that base mistress and the brothel's law.
That Virtue brave, Sobriety, bemoaned
This crime: her friends withdrawing on the right, 345
A band unconquered lost without bloodshed.
The standard of the cross she had advanced
That noble leader fixes in the ground
And rallies her inconstant troops with words
Of mingled pleading and severe reproach: 350

'What madness touches your disordered minds?
Where do you rush?[47] To whom do you submit?
What chains do you, for shame, desire to wear
On warlike arms, these yellow wreaths entwined
With lilies fair, these crowns of dark red flowers? 355
Are you resolved to yield to bonds like these
Your hands inured to war, bind thus your arms;
To let the golden coif, with yellow band
Restraining virile locks, drink up the oil,
When once the sign upon your brows was traced, 360
A royal unction and eternal chrism;
To sweep your footprints with a trailing robe,[48]
To clothe your limbs with flowing gowns of silk,
When once Faith wove for you with skillful hand
A lasting tunic, giving to cleansed hearts, 365
Through her reborn, a shield impervious;
Then to nocturnal feasts, where tankards spill

---
47 Cf. Vergil, *Aeneid* 12.313.
48 Cf. Vergil, *Georgics* 3.59.

Their foaming wastes of wine, while ladles drip
On boards, where couches are with liquor wet
And carvings are still moist with ancient dew? 370
Do you forget the thirst in desert lands,
The spring vouchsafed your fathers from the rock,
Which mystic rod drew forth from sundered stone?[49]
Did not angelic food upon the tents
Of your ancestors fall,[50] of which more blessed 375
The people from Christ's body now partake?[51]
You, at this banquet fed, indulgence drags
To Sensuality's vile drunken den,
And soldier neither wrath nor heathen gods
Could force to yield, a dancing girl has swayed! 380
Stand, I pray, mindful of yourselves and Christ.
Think of your race, your fame, your God and King,
Your Lord. You, Juda's noble seed, have come
From line of mighty princes reaching down
To God's own Mother through whom He was Man. 385
Let holy David's fame your noble spirits rouse,
One in unceasing tasks of war engaged.
Let Samuel rouse you, who forbids that spoils
From a rich foe be touched, nor lets the king
Uncircumcised live on, lest he might force 390
The peaceful victor to renew the war.[52]
He thinks it crime to spare the captive king,
But you wish to be vanquished and succumb.
Repent, if you have any fear of God,
That you have followed this temptation sweet; 395
If you repent, it is no deadly sin.
For Jonathan repented that he broke
The solemn fast by tasting honey smeared
Upon his rod, when charmed by his desire

---
49 Cf. Exod. 17.3-6.
50 Cf. Exod. 16.14,15.
51 The Holy Eucharist, of which the manna was a type.
52 Cf. 1 Kings 15.33.

Of power, the youth transgressed the sacred law.⁵³ 400
Since he repented, we weep not his lot,
And no harsh sentence stained his father's ax.
Lo, I, Sobriety, if you join me,
Will now to all the Virtues show a way
For Sensuality and her great train 405
To suffer punishment from Christ the Judge.'

So speaking, she uplifts a crucifix
And thrusts the holy wood against the reins
Of the raging team. The savage steeds take fright
At its extended arms and gleaming crest, 410
And in blind fear they rush in headlong flight
Adown the precipice. The charioteer
In vain pulls in the reins and borne along,
She soils her hair with dust. Thrown out, she falls
Beneath entangling wheels and stops the car, 415
Her mangled body serving as the brake.
Sobriety hurls from the cliff a stone
And gives the death-blow to her lying there.
As chance gave to the leader this strong bolt,
Who bears no weapons but her warlike sign,⁵⁴ 420
Chance drives the stone to crush the breathing mouth
And with the hollow palate mix the lips.
The teeth within are loosened, and the tongue
All mangled, fills the throat with clots of blood.
The throat rebels at this unwonted food 425
And then spews up the lumps of broken bones.
'Drink now your blood after your many cups,'
The maiden chides, 'let this be your grim fare
In place of all the sweets of your past life.
Let death's unsavory taste and this vile draught 430
Turn all the pleasures of your life to gall.'

---

53 Cf. 1 Kings 14.24 ff.
54 Cf. Vergil, *Aeneid* 8.683.

Then at their leader's death, the scattered line
Atremble flees. First, Jest and Petulance
Their cymbals throw away, for with such arms
They played at war, intending wounds with noise.   435
Love turns his back in flight, and pale with fear,
He leaves behind his poisoned darts, his bow
And quiver from his shoulders falling down.
Vainglorious Pomp of her proud flowing robe
Is stripped; the wreaths of Charm are torn away   440
And from her neck and head the gold is loosed,
While hostile Discord scatters all her gems.
Through thorny briers Pleasure freely goes
With feet all bruised, because a greater power
Makes her endure the bitter flight, and fear   445
Steels tender soles to bear the torturing way.
Wherever the column turns its frightened course[55]
Lie objects lost, a hairpin, ribbons, bands,
A brooch, veil, bodice, necklace, diadem.
Sobriety, with her whole army, scorns   450
These spoils and tramples these cursed stumbling blocks
Beneath her virtuous feet, nor does she gaze
Upon this tempting plunder with delight.

They say that Avarice, clothed in ample robe,
Seized all of worth that Sensuality   455
Had left behind, gazing with open mouth
Upon the pretty toys and picking up
The golden fragments in the heaps of sand.
Not satisfied with pockets full, she joys
To cram with sordid gain her money-bags,   460
Which in her robe she hides with her left hand,
While with the right she gathers up the spoils
And fills her brazen claws with filthy loot.
With her go as companions diverse fiends,
Care, Hunger, Fear, Distress, Pallor, and Fraud,   465

---
[55] Cf. *ibid.* 11.762.

Intrigue, Deceit, Craft, Sleeplessness, and Greed.[56]
And all the while, like ravening wolves, the Crimes,
Fed on the sable milk of Avarice,
Go prowling round the wide, unbroken plain.
Then if a soldier sees his brother's helm   470
Agleam with tawny gems, he does not fear
To draw his sword and to strike off his head
That he may snatch the jewels from the crown.
And if a son sees lying on the field
His father's body, he strips off as spoils   475
The bright gold-studded belt and bloody arms:
Thus civil strife despoils its next of kin,
Unsated greed its dear ones does not spare,
And impious hunger robs its own offspring.

Such carnage Avarice, conqueror of the world, 480
Spread through the nations,[57] laying thousands low
By various wounds: one with his eyes gouged out,
And blinded, she permits, as in dark night,
To wander over many stumbling blocks
And never test the dangers with a staff.   485
Another through his sight she lures by show
Of something fair, and as he covets it,
He is entrapped, unheeding, by her stroke
And winces at the sword-thrust in his heart.
A multitude she drives to open fires,   490
Not suffering them to shun the seething gold,
Which, doomed to burn with it, the swindler seeks.
The human race, all mortals she ensnares
And leads to ruin, nor is there on the earth
A vice more fierce, one that involves all men 495
In such bloodshed, condemning them to hell.
With her own hand, if it can be believed,[58]

---
56 Cf. *ibid.* 6.274-281.
57 Cf. *ibid.* 10.602.
58 Cf. *ibid.* 6.173.

She dared to tempt the very priests of God,
The leaders in the foremost line,[59] who fought
And cheered the Virtues with loud trumpet blasts.   500
She might have stained her sword in their chaste blood
Had not the warrior, Reason, true comrade
Of Levi's sons, before them raised her shield
And from them warded off the foe's onslaught.
They stand with help of Reason safe, they stand   505
Immune from every storm and brave of heart;
A few the spear of Avarice slightly grazed
With skin-deep wounds. The foul plague was amazed
To see her darts rebound from their pure throats,
And groaning, she begins with frenzied words: 510
'We lose the fight, alas, our might has lost
Its wonted strength, our power to hurt grows weak,
Which once was wont to pierce the hearts of men
With force invincible; for man has not
So iron a nature that he can resist   515
Our bronze or be indifferent to our gold.
We have led every heart to ruin;[60] the kind,
Rough, hard, learned and unlearned, the dull, the wise,
Pure and impure, have been within our grasp.
Whatever Styx hides in its floods, alone   520
We carried off, to us hell owes the hordes
Held in its depths; what ages spin is ours,
What earth confounds, its mad turmoil, is ours.
How comes it that our well-known glory wanes,
And fortune ridicules our useless arms?   525
The yellow image on the gleaming coin
Is worthless to the followers of Christ,
Money and wealth are paltry in their sight.
Why these sophistic airs? Did we not gain
A victory over Iscariot, one great[61]   530

---
59 Cf. *ibid.* 7.531.
60 Cf. Vergil, *Georgics* 3.480.
61 Cf. Matt. 26.14,15.

Among the friends of God, His guest at meat,
When, false, he put his hand into the dish,[62]
And fell upon our weapon, having bought
A noxious field with price of his Friend's blood,
Doomed to atonement by a broken neck?[63]   535
And Jericho had seen in her own ruin
Our hand's control, when conquering Achan fell.[64]
Renowned for bloodshed, proud of leveling walls,
He fell a victim to the enemy's gold
When from the dust he gleaned the stuff accurst   540
And snatched the mournful plunder from the ruins.
His tribe did not avail, nor his descent
From Juda, founder of the race of Christ[65]
And patriarch blessed in his noble scion.
Let those who imitate his race accept   545
A similar form of death and punishment.
Why do I hesitate to circumvent
The stock of Juda or of Aaron high[66]
Since I am not a match for them in war?
What matter whether we win by arms or fraud?'   550
With these words she puts off her fiendish look
And frightful arms, and puts on honest mien:[67]
She now becomes a Virtue, stern of face
And dress,[68] and called Frugality, who loves
To pinch and save, as though she would seize nought   555
And had a right to praise for what she feigned.
Bellona[69] clothes herself in similar garb,
As thrifty Virtue, not a greedy plague,
And with a veil of piety she hides
Her snaky locks, that the white cloak may mask   560

---

62 Cf. Mark 14.20.
63 Cf. Acts 1.18.
64 Cf. Jos. 7.1,21,25.
65 Cf. Jos. 7.16.
66 Cf. Num. 3.6-10.
67 Cf. Vergil, *Aeneid* 7.415-416.
68 Cf. Juvenal 14.109-111.
69 The Roman war-goddess.

Her rage and fury, and she may excuse
Under the name of love of her offspring
Her theft and pillage and rapacity.
In such deceptive likenesses she blinds
The hearts of men, who heed the deadly fiend[70]   565
And, deeming her a Virtue, are ensnared
As easy victims in the Fury's toils.
Their leaders dazed, their battle lines confused,
The Virtues wavered, by the monster's form
Misled and doubtful whether she was friend   570
Or foe. The deadly creature's double shape
Confounds their sight and makes them hesitate,
When Mercy suddenly dashes on the field[71]
And wroth, takes up the fight in their behalf,
Last in the battle line, but destined soon,   575
Alone, to terminate the dreadful war.
From off her shoulders every weight was cast,
As quick she moved, of cloak and pack relieved,[72]
Once cramped by riches and hard money bags,
But freed by kindly pity on the poor,   580
Whom she had aided with ancestral wealth.
Rich now in faith, she eyed her empty purse
And counted up her lasting wealth and gain.[73]
At sight of that brave Virtue, Avarice quaked,
And as one paralyzed, she stood unmoved   585
And sure of death.[74] For by what trickery
Could she entice one who had spurned the world
To love again the gold she had despised?
The Virtue falls upon the trembling Vice
With might of clutching arms and, strangling her,   590
She breaks her dry and bloodless throat: the arms,
Locked underneath her chin, compress her jaws

---

70 Cf. Claudian, *De raptu Pros.* 1.37.
71 Cf. Claudian, *In Eutropium* 2.549-550.
72 Cf. Vergil, *Eclogues* 9.65.
73 Cf. Matt. 19.21,29.
74 Cf. Vergil, *Aeneid* 4.564.

And take away her life without a wound,
For when the channel of her breath is blocked,
She suffers death enclosed within her veins. 595
With knee and foot pressed on the struggling Vice,
The victor stabs her ribs and heaving sides,[75]
Then from the body takes away the spoils:
Bits of unpolished gold not yet refined
In fiery forges, purses eaten up 600
By gnawing worms, coins green with rust,
Things hoarded long, she to the needy gives,
And with the captured booty helps the poor.
Then glancing round with joyful countenance,
She fervently exhorts the mighty host: 605
'Cease fighting, ye upright, and lay aside
Your arms. The cause of all our woe lies slain.[76]
With lust for gain now dead, the saints may rest.
To wish for nothing more than need demands
Is rest supreme, with simple food and dress 610
To feed and clothe our bodies and to seek
No more than is prescribed by nature's wants.
When going on a journey, take no purse,[77]
Nor of a second tunic think, and be
Not anxious for the morrow,[78] lest for food 615
The belly lack. Our daily bread returns
With every sun. Does any bird take thought
Of tomorrow, certain to be fed by God?[79]
The fowls of little value trust that food
Will fail not, sparrows for a farthing sold,[80] 620
Have certain faith that God will care for them.
Dost thou, God's care and image of His Christ,
Fear thy Creator will abandon thee?

---

75 Cf. *ibid.* 9.431.
76 Cf. *ibid.* 6.93; 11.480.
77 Cf. Matt. 10.10; Mark 6.8,9; Luke 9.3; 22.35.
78 Cf. Matt. 6.34.
79 Cf. Matt. 6.26.
80 Cf. Matt. 10.29.

Fear not, O men! He who gives life, gives food.
Seek the light-bringing food of heavenly lore, 625
Which fosters hope of everlasting life,[81]
Unmindful of the body: He who made
Our frame will furnish food for all our needs.'

Care vanished at these words,[82] Fear, Toil, and Rage,
And Crime and Fraud that heavenly Faith denies 630
Were driven from the land. Then kindly Peace,
The foe now put to flight, drives War away;
Fear is dispelled and fighting gear unclasped.
The flowing robes fall to the warriors' feet,[83]
And peaceful modesty checks their rapid steps. 635
The trumpets now are silent, swords are sheathed,
The dust subsides upon the field, the day
Returns with bright and cloudless face, and light
From heaven shines resplendent to the view.
The squadrons, joyful at the battle's end, 640
Saw that the Thunderer smiled upon their ranks,
That Christ, rejoicing in their victory,
Was opening up for them His Father's home.[84]
Concord gives signal to bear back to camp
The conquering eagles[85] and take to their tents. 645
Never did troops make such a splendid show
As when in double lines she led them forth,
The section of footsoldiers chanting psalms,
And that of mounted warriors singing hymns.
So conquering Israel sang when looking back[86] 650
Upon the yawning gulf of the rabid sea,
As now they trod dry-foot the farther shore,
And as the mass of water grazed their heels

---
81 Cf. Matt. 6.23.
82 Cf. Vergil, *Aeneid* 6.382.
83 Cf. *ibid.* 1.404.
84 Cf. Apoc. 3.21.
85 Cf. Lucan 5.238.
86 Cf. Exod. 15.1-19.

And in its ebbing flood engulfed the host
Of swarthy dwellers on the Nile, while fish 655
Now swam again in flooded hollow bays,
And headlong billows overspread the sands.
God's people their melodious timbrels beat[87]
To celebrate the great and wondrous work
Of the Omnipotent, when having cut 660
The waves and stayed the winds, He raised up banks
Of water and checked the thronging hordes.
So when the race of Vices was subdued,
The Virtues sang melodious hymns and psalms.

The band had reached the portals of the camp[88] 665
With narrow access through the double doors.
Here rises an unforeseen enemy,
A cunning Vice that strikes at placid Peace
And mars her triumph with a sudden blow.
Concord, surrounded by the close-packed throng, 670
When safe within the walls she has set foot,
Receives in her left side a treacherous wound
Made by a lurking Vice, although the mail
She wore upon her body, with its chains
Of iron, repelled the dart, nor did the links, 675
Joined firmly with their rigid knots, permit
The steel to penetrate deep in the flesh.
And yet an open seam allowed the sword
To pass through with a trivial puncture, where
The last scale of the cuirass joined the belt. 680
A crafty warrior of the losing side
Struck this blow, with the victors off their guard.
For when the Vices had been overthrown,
Discord our ranks had entered as a friend.
Far off amid the tumult of the field 685
Lay her torn robe and scourge of many snakes,

---
87 Cf. Exod. 15.21.
88 Cf. Vergil, *Aeneid* 6.45.

While she herself, with crown of olive leaves
Responded joyfully to the festive choir.[89]
Beneath her cloak a dagger she concealed
To strike thee, Concord, greatest Virtue, thee   690
Of all the band; but she was not allowed
To pierce the vitals of thy sacred frame,
Only to wound the skin with slightest touch.[90]
'What is this?' cries the Virtue thus disturbed.
'What hostile hand is hidden here, which hurts   695
Our triumph and in midst of joy strikes?
What use to have subdued the Passions fierce
And brought the holy back, with Vices dead,
If under Peace a Virtue falls?' The ranks
Turned mournful eyes upon the blood that stained[91]   700
Her coat of mail. Then fear betrays the foe
As she stands nigh; for pallid cheeks reveal
Her guilty knowledge of the daring deed,
And hand and face quail at discovery.
Round her the Virtues throng with swords unsheathed[92] 705
And breathless ask her race, her name, her home,
And faith, what God she venerates and by
What nation sent. She pale with fear replies:
'Discord is my first name and Heresy
My second. God to me is various,   710
Now lesser or now greater, now twofold,
Now simple; when I scoff at his divinity,
He is a phantom or the soul within.
My teacher is Belial, my home the world.'
No longer Faith, the Virtues' queen, could bear[93]   715
This blasphemy, but checked the monster's words
And closed the vocal passage with her spear,
Transfixing the foul tongue with its firm point.

---

89 Cf. *ibid.* 8.702-703.
90 Cf. *ibid.* 1.737.
91 Cf. *ibid.* 11.812.
92 Cf. *ibid.* 12.662-663.
93 Cf. Ovid, *Metamorphoses* 3.487.

Hands without number rend the deadly beast;
Each one takes for herself a piece to fling   720
Into the air, or give to dogs, or throw
To carrion crows, or into sewers cast,[94]
Or to the monsters of the sea consign.
The whole corpse torn to bits is thrown to beasts;
Thus Heresy perishes, all her members rent.[95]   725

Now that prosperity has been restored,
Now that the people are at peace again
And all the Virtues, safe within the walls,
Can now in leisure find relief from care,[96]
A rostrum is constructed on a hill   730
In middle of the camp, and this high place
Serves as a watchtower, whence the eye may view
Afar on every side what lies below.
True Faith and, likewise, Concord, sisters vowed
In sacred kinship for the love of Christ,   735
Ascend the height,[97] and then the holy pair,
Dear to each other and with equal power,
Together take their stand upon the stage[98]
And bid the populous throng to gather round.
From every corner of the camp they rush;   740
No portion of the Soul keeps out of sight,
Hiding itself in shameful idleness
In some retreat of flesh; with flaps drawn back,
All tents are open that no inmate may
Lie snoring loudly in secluded ease.   745
With ears intent, the concourse waits to hear
Why Concord calls the victors after war,
Or what rule Faith may to the Virtues give.

---
94 Cf. Columella 10.85.
95 Cf. Juvenal 3.259-260.
96 In lines 727-730, Bergman accepts the version found in Ms.A and others. In this translation the variant version, quoted in Bergman's note, page 203, and accepted by Thomson, is followed.
97 Cf. Claudian, *In Eutropium* 1.311.
98 Cf. Claudian, *De bello Gildonico* 425.

With these words, Concord first breaks forth in speech:
'Abundant glory now has come to you, 750
O faithful children of the Father and
Of Christ the Lord. You have in fierce conflict
Wiped out the cruel demons that beset
With fire and sword the city of the saints.[99]
The nation's peace rests on benevolence 755
In field and town. A state divided falls,[100]
And lack of peace within brings war without.
Take care, my warriors, lest dissensions rise[101]
Within our souls, lest heresy spring up
From hidden discords, for a divided will 760
A fickle heart confounds with hostile views.
May love unite our minds, one aim inspire
Our lives: for without union nought is strong.
As Jesus reconciled mankind to God
And to His Father joined our mortal frame, 765
That flesh might not be parted from the Spirit,
And that God might be both, so let one mind
Unite us all in body and in soul.
Peace crowns the Virtue's work,[102] peace is the fruit
Of toil, reward for war and peril braved. 770
In peace stars shine, in peace the earth stands fast.
Without peace nought is pleasing unto God.
No gift brought to the altar is approved,[103]
If hate of brother dwells within thy heart,
And if for Christ a martyr thou shouldst leap 775
Into the flames[104] whilst thou an unkind wish
Dost keep, to have for Jesus given thy life
Will profit not, for peace is merit's ground:
It is not proud, a brother envies not,[105]

---

99 Cf. Vergil, *Aeneid* 10.232.
100 Cf. Matt. 12.25.
101 Cf. 1 Cor. 1.10.
102 Cf. Claudian, *Laus Serenae* 12.
103 Cf. Matt. 5.24.
104 Cf. 1 Cor. 13.3.
105 Cf. 1 Cor 13.4-8.

Endures all things with calm, believes all things, 780
It never grieves at wrongs, forgives affronts,
It joys to pardon ere the end of day[106]
And worries lest the sun leave wrath behind.
He who would offer holocausts to God
Let him first offer peace; no sacrifice 785
To Christ is sweeter; with its fragrance pure
This gift alone is pleasing in His sight.
God gives the snow-white doves skill to discern[107]
The feathered serpent in his peaceful dress
Of downy plumage, when with harmless birds 790
He mingles; so the wolf with bloody jaws
In clothing of a sheep conceals himself[108]
When he spreads deadly ruin among the lambs.
Plotinus and Arius thus hide themselves,[109]
Wolves wild and fierce.[110] Our recent jeopardy 795
And bloodshed, though skin-deep, reveal the power
Of a furtive hand.' Stunned by the bitter blow,[111]
The whole array of Virtues gave a groan.
Then noble Faith advanced and spoke these words:
'In this blest hour, let mourning cease. Concord 800
Was hurt, but Faith has been upheld. With Faith
Concord stands safe and laughs at petty wounds.[112]
She is my shield, her rescue bans all grief.
After this war one work remains for us,
O leaders, that which Solomon achieved, 805
The peaceful scion and the unarmed heir[113]
Of a warlike realm, whose father's weary hand
Was sullied by the ardent blood of kings.
The blood effaced, a temple is upraised

---

106 Cf. Eph. 4.26.
107 Cf. Matt. 10.16.
108 Cf. Matt. 7.15.
109 Heretics of the fourth century.
110 Cf. Acts 20.29.
111 Cf. Vergil, *Aeneid* 5.700.
112 Cf. *ibid.* 9.262.
113 Cf. 3 Kings 5.3-5.

And golden altar, house sublime of Christ.[114]   810
Jerusalem then by her temple crowned,
Received her God, now that the wandering ark
Upon the marble altar found repose.[115]
In our camp let a sacred temple rise,
That God may in its sanctuary dwell.   815
What profits it to have repelled the hosts
Of earth-born Vices, if the Son of Man,
From heaven descending, enters the body cleansed,
But unadorned and not a temple fair?
Thus far we have engaged in fierce conflict: 820
Now let white-vestured Peace perform her tasks,
And youth unarmed build up a sacred house.'

So speaking, with her friend Concord, the queen[116]
Descended and began to measure out
The temple on foundations newly laid.   825
Her golden reed surveys the distances,[117]
That all four sides may square and joints be straight
And no uneven corner may destroy
The graceful plan by lack of symmetry.
One square lies on the side of dawn lit up   830
By triple doors; three doors lead to the south;[118]
Three entrances are offered on the west,
And toward the north the lofty hall presents
As many more.[119] No building stone is there;
A solid gem, in which an opening   835
Has been cut, frames the door with gleaming arch,
And one stone forms the entrance vestibule.
Inscribed in gold on top of these doorways,
The names, twice six, of the apostles shine.[120]

---
114 Cf. 3 Kings 6.22.
115 Cf. 3 Kings 8.6.
116 Cf. Vergil, *Aeneid* 2.790; 6.628.
117 Cf. Apoc. 21.15-17.
118 Cf. Apoc. 21.13.
119 Cf. Vergil, *Aeneid* 8.262.
120 Cf. Apoc. 21.14.

The Spirit by these scrolls attracts the soul   840
And fills the heart with holy sentiments;
It enters through three doors this inner shrine
In each of the four ages of man's life
And gilds the holy place with chaste desires;
Whether it be in childhood's early dawn,   845
The heat of ardent youth, the full sunlight
Of man's maturity, or wintry chill
Of feeble age, three names present themselves
On each of the four sides, which by the King
Have been inscribed to His disciples twelve.   850
Nay more, an equal number of rich gems
Set in the walls, shine brightly, and the light
Pours forth from their clear depths in living hues.
A chrysolite ingrained with gold is set[121]
Between a sapphire and a beryl green,   855
And their joint glow gives rise to varied charms.
Here a chalcedony is steeped with light
From neighboring hyacinth; for that dark stone
Shone nearby with its limpid purple depths.
The amethyst imbues the sardony,   860
The jasper and topaz, the sardius.
Among these, emeralds shine like meadows green,
And verdant light flows forth in billowing waves.
Thou too, bright chrysoprase, dost gild this shrine,
And thy star joins the other glittering stones.   865
The heavy cables of the pulley creaked
As to the heights it raised the massive gems.
Within the shrine a lofty hall is built
Upheld by seven pillars, crystal clear,[122]
Whose capitals are topped with milk-white stone   870
Cut into cones, with lower edge upturned
And curved in likeness of a shell, a pearl
Which Faith had for a thousand talents bought,

---

121 Cf. Apoc. 21.19,20.
122 Cf. Prov. 9.1; Vergil, *Aeneid* 1.637.

Derived from auction of her property.[123]
Here Wisdom dwells, and from a lofty throne, 875
Directs the government of all the realm,
And issues laws for saving all mankind.
She holds a sceptre not by artist made,
But living rod that severed from the tree,[124]
Though nurtured by no sap from earthly soil, 880
Still puts forth verdant leaves and twines
With blood-red roses lilies white and fair
That never bend their heads on shriveled stems.
This sceptre was foreshadowed by the rod[125]
Of Aaron, which from lifeless bark put forth 885
A flower of tender beauty full of hope
And new shoots sprouting from the arid branch.[126]

Eternal thanks we give to Thee, O Christ,
Most gentle Teacher, and with pious lips
We sing Thy praise[127]—for sin has stained our hearts. 890
Thou hast willed us to know the hidden foes
Within the body and the soul's grim strife.
Conflicting passions in our heart, we know,
Wage ceaseless wars with outcomes various:
Our souls now grow in goodness, and again 895
When virtues are subdued, they are enslaved
And give themselves to shameful sins, which lead
To loss of their salvation and their ruin.
How often have we felt our soul grow warm[128]
With love of God, when vices were repulsed; 900
How often felt our hearts grow cold and yield
To sin after this joy! Within our frame
Wars rage,[129] and human nature rises up

---
123 Cf. Matt. 13.45,46.
124 Cf. Vergil, *Aeneid* 12.208.
125 Cf. *ibid.* 3.286.
126 Cf. Num. 17.8; Heb. 9.4.
127 Cf. Vergil, *Aeneid* 3.118.
128 Cf. Ovid, *Metamorphoses* 2.641.
129 Cf. Vergil, *Aeneid* 6.86; Statius, *Thebaid* 4.601; 6.457.

In fierce revolt,[130] for flesh formed of the mire
Weighs heavy on the spirit; but the pure spirit,   905
Formed by the breath of God, rebels inside
Its prison, and the body's foulness spurns:
Diverse in spirit, light with darkness wars,[131]
And our two natures are at variance,
Till Christ our God is present with His grace   910
And all the jewels of the virtues sets
In shrine made pure; then where sin reigned He builds
His temple with its gilded halls, and weaves
From Valor proved adornments for the soul
Where Wisdom will always delight to reign.   915

---

130 Cf. Vergil, *Georgics* 2.459; Statius, *Thebaid* 11.100.
131 Cf. Gal. 5.17.

AGAINST SYMMACHUS

(CONTRA SYMMACHUM)

Book One

AGAINST SYMMACHUS

Book One

Preface

Paul, the herald of God, who with his holy pen
First subdued the untamed hearts of the gentile tribes,
Sowing knowledge of Christ with his precepts benign
Over barbarous lands following savage ways,
That uncivilized folk heathenish rites might spurn   5
And arrive at a firm knowledge of one true God,
Of old happened to be driven by tempest dark
Through a turbulent sea in an unstable ship
And braved furious winds threatening to sink the craft.[1]
When the hand of the Lord calmed the cerulean flood,[2]   10
Stilling the boisterous waves, bidding them sink to rest,
Into harbor the ship glided while still afloat,
And secure on the wet shore disembarked the crew
All benumbed by the cold drizzle of freezing rain.[3]
Then, still shivering, they hastily gathered twigs,   15
Arid branches from brush nigh to the sandy beach,
Whence they kindled a fire blazing up rapidly;
As each piled on the flames bundles of fagots dry,
He took heart from the warmth shed from the glowing pyre.
While Paul busied himself gathering the shriveled boughs[4] 20
And then piling them high upon the blazing heap,
His hand, heedless, he thrust into the pile of wood,

---
1 Cf. Acts 27, 28.
2 Cf. Ovid, *Metamorphoses* 2.528.
3 Cf. Vergil, *Georgics* 3.279.
4 Cf. Acts 28.2-6.

Where a slumbering asp, lying benumbed with cold,
Had encircled the twigs with its entwining coils.
When the viper grew warm close to the smoking fire[5]   25
And its neck was relaxed, which had been stiff with frost,
Fierce it darted its head turning about with ease,
And soon struck at the saint's hand with ferocious teeth.
Paul was stricken by fear when he upraised the snake,
Clinging fast to his hand wounded by mordant fangs.   30
Others cried out in awe, thinking the deadly bane
Was already diffused through the now livid skin.
The Apostle did not quail at the sudden blow
But undaunted he stood facing the peril grim.
He then raising his eyes, looked up to heaven above,[6]   35
Softly murmuring Christ's name in his inmost heart,[7]
And the serpent shook off, tossing it far away.
Now the reptile cast off, beating the frigid air,
Opened its vicious mouth and soon released its fangs.
Quick the virulent blood flowed from the saint's right hand,   40
As though never a wound harrowed the smarting flesh,
And the viperous fluid dried up and disappeared.
The Apostle's strong thrust sent the nefarious snake
Whirling into the fire, where it was burned to death.

Today, after the fierce tempests of raging seas,   45
Whereon Wisdom's frail bark tottered in savage winds
When she drifted with fear under ungodly kings
And could scarcely advance even with hoisted sails,
When by storms of the world passengers were distressed,
As through turbulent waves floated the stricken craft,   50
Again has her wise law suffered a bitter wound.
For a viper had been shrouded in secrecy
And its virulent head hitherto had not raised,
Content to be inclosed deep in its hidden lair

---
[5] Cf. Ovid, *Metamorphoses* 2.173-175.
[6] Cf. *ibid.* 5.503.
[7] Cf. *ibid.* 2.203.

And a silence profound keep in its dark retreat. 55
While Impiety lay crouched in this hiding place,
Stiff and sluggish with cold, forthwith its ire was roused,
And embittered by hate, Justice's right hand it struck.
Ah, how all but in vain has been the voyage rough
Of the Catholic bark, guided by holy writ, 60
Which by Paul was sent forth into the various lands!
Scarce had she come to rest, safe in a tranquil port,
After victories won over a thousand storms,
Scarce had anchors been made fast with the mooring ropes
And the travelers debarked, sure on the solid ground, 65
When the dangerous plague suddenly showed its head.
While they kindled hot fires thus to abate the cold
And to ease their fatigue, while in the flames they burned
The abortive offshoots, branches unsound and bare
From the vine of the Faith, heavy and overgrown, 70
That the mass of wild twigs, dense and disorderly,
Might be rid of the foul growth of idolatry,
The caress of the warmth brought the vile pest to life.
Then the serpent began creeping around again,
Proudly shaking its head, subtle in eloquence, 75
But an obdurate hand, reckless of threatened wound,[8]
Rendered empty and null all its impassioned words,[9]
And its venomous spirit flowed from its mouth in vain,
Turned aside by the shield borne by the Christian souls.

O Savior of the race founded by Romulus, 80
Who Thy pardoning grace grantest to fallen men,
Thou who savest mankind as Thy creation dear
And with merciful hand quickly dost raise it up,
Have compassion, I pray, now if it be Thy will,
On this man who has plunged into a deep abyss. 85
He unknowingly breathes haughty impiety
And in ignorance clings firmly to errors false.

---
8 Cf. Vergil, *Aeneid* 11.639; Statius, *Thebaid* 9.872.
9 Reference to the oratorical powers of Symmachus.

I beg Thee to ordain that he shall not be hurled
Headlong into the fire where he will burn always.

I thought that Rome, once sick with pagan vice,
Had purged herself by now of old disease
And that no trace remained since our good prince[1]
Had eased her grievous pains by healing laws.
But since the plague, of late revived, torments   5
The sons of Romulus, we must beg God's help,
Lest Rome now fall into the olden mire,
And princely robes be stained with smoke and blood.
Did that great father of his country, lord
Of the whole world,[2] do nought when he forbade   10
The old belief that gods roamed in the air,
And worship, in the place of Deity,
Of the Almighty Father's handiwork?
He dreaded lest the nation's moral wound[3]
Might form a scar, healed only on the skin   15
And fostering deep below the sutured welt,
Due to the surgeon's fault, a hidden sore
Corroded with decaying purulence.
He strove man's higher nature to revive
And to instruct the soul, cleansed of the plague,   20
How to keep safe from toxic ills within.
The remedy of tyrants heretofore
Had been to see what measures would fulfill
The present needs, with no concern beyond.
Alas, how ill they served this land, how ill   25
The senators, whom they allowed to sink
Into the pit with Jove and lesser gods.[4]
This prince has spread his rule to future times
By striving to assure the common weal.

---

[1] The emperor, Theodosius I, forbade pagan worship in the year 391.
[2] Cf. Ovid, *Fasti* 2.127-132.
[3] Cf. Claudian, *De cons. Stil.* 2.205; Paulinus of Nola, *Poema* 19.215-218.
[4] Cf. Ovid, *Metamorphoses* 1.173.

A learned man says happily indeed: 30
'The nation would be blest abundantly
If kings were wise or wise men ruled as kings.'[5]
Is our prince not of those who wear the crown
And truths of heavenly wisdom advocate?
All mankind and the togaed race rejoice[6]
To have in him a leader wise; Rome thrives,
For justice reigns: obey the chief who holds
The scepter! He commands you to shake off
The superstitious errors of your sires,
To know no god but Him who rules all things 40
And shaped the vast dimensions of the world.

Do we believe that Saturn better ruled[7]
Our Latin forebears, he who trained rude minds
And savage hearts with mandates such as these:
'I am a god, I came a fugitive; 45
Give me asylum; hide an aged god
Thrust out by a faithless son. Here will I lurk
And name of *Latin* give to race and land.[8]
A pruning hook of iron I shall forge
To trim your vines, and I shall build a town, 50
Known as Saturnia, on your river banks.[9]
You shall devote a grove and altar there
To honor me—for I am son of heaven.'
Their witless children chiseled gods from bronze,
Whose tombs we know are in their country seen, 55
Whom that outcast in shape of horse begot[10]
And brought to Italy: for he was first
To woo the Tuscan maids as fictive god.

---
5 Cf. Plato, *Republic* 5.473d; Cicero, *Ad Quintum* 1.1.29.
6 Cf. Vergil, *Aeneid*, 1.282.
7 Cf. Minucius Felix, *Octavius* 21.4-7 (Vol. 10, this series); also Tertullian, *Apology* 10.6-11 (Vol. 10, this series); Cyprian, *Quod idoli dii non sunt* 2 (Vol. 36, this series).
8 Cf. Vergil, *Aeneid* 8.322-323.
9 Cf. *ibid.* 357-358.
10 Cf. Vergil, *Georgics* 3.92-95.

Olympian Jupiter, baser than his sire,[11]
Laconian women soiled with shameful lust: 60
Now carrying off his loved one on a bull;
Now as a swan, with feathers soft as down,
Singing the rapturous notes of its death song
To lure a maid that she may bear his love;
Now when the doors were barred with heavy bolts, 65
As a rich lover, breaking hollow tiles
And pouring through the roof a shower of gold
Into the bosom of his paramour;
Now with his armor-bearer helping him
Embracing Ganymede with lustful arms 70
And rousing thus his sister's jealous wrath.
The source of all this ill is that dull folk
Saw in the outcast's reign a golden age,
And that the wily Jupiter devised
A thousand forms of guile and trickery, 75
Changing his skin and face to make men think
He was a bull, an eagle, or a swan,
Or gold infused into a maiden's breast.
For what would not such ignorant men believe,
Whose lives were spent with herds and savage beasts, 80
Whose minds were not endowed with sense divine?
To any myth that wanton knave conceived
The hapless people gave a ready ear.

The reign of Jove was followed by an age
Which made the hardy rustics slaves to sin. 85
Men ignorant of theft were taught this art
By Mercury, Maia's son.[12] Now he is deemed
A mighty god whose shrewdness turned out thieves.
Skilled in Thessalian magic, as they tell,
He called the spirits of the dead to life[13] 90

---
11 Cf. Tertullian, *Apology* 21.8 (Vol. 10, this series); also Cyprian, *Ad Donatum* 8 (Vol. 36, this series).
12 Cf. Vergil, *Aeneid* 1.297.
13 Cf. *ibid.* 4.242-243.

By power of his wand and nullified
Dominion of Cocytus over death
By raising up the shades or plunging them
Into the depths below. He had both skills
And armed his hand with heinous twofold crime; 95
With mumbled magic he knew how to raise
The spirits and cast a spell on dust entombed,
While others he astutely robbed of life.
The simple wondered at his vicious craft
And deemed him more than man, borne through the
    clouds 100
And on winged feet traversing lively winds.

Among the gods there stands one forged of bronze,
A man of Greece, who shines on Numa's height.[14]
He was the lord of well-tilled fields and famed
For teeming gardens, but a libertine, 105
Who full of burning passion used to plague
The country women and ensconce himself
Amid the willow groves and hedges dense;
Urged on by lust and ready for misdeeds
He gave no respite to his fiery blood. 110
This famous god came from the Hellespont[15]
And brought to Italy's gardens his base rites;
Receiving yearly bowls of milk and cakes,[16]
He guards the rural vineyards of Sabine,
And with his bough is shameful to behold. 115

The love that Hercules felt for a boy
Upon the cross-banks of the Argo raged,
The while beneath Nemean skin he hid[17]
His lust and for lost Hylas searched in vain.
Now dancing priests of the Pinarian house 120

---
14 Priapus, the protector of gardens; cf. Ovid, *Fasti*, 6.319-333.
15 Cf. Vergil, *Georgics* 4.111.
16 Cf. Vergil, *Eclogues* 7.33.
17 Cf. Vergil, *Aeneid* 8.295.

Frequent his temple on the Aventine.[18]

A Theban youth, who conquered India,[19]
Is made a god and triumphs wantonly;
Proud of his gold and spoils from captured lands,[20]
He gives himself to revels with his crew   125
And steeps himself in rich Falernian wine,
Besprinkling from his foaming jeweled cup[21]
The dewy backs of his ferocious team.
To Bacchus now a goat is sacrificed[22]
On every altar, and they gnaw green snakes   130
Who Bromius would appease, as satyrs did
In drunken madness then before the king,
And maenads, too, in frenzy, I believe,
When wine inflamed and drove them into sin.
With this wild troop the drunken debauchee   135
Finds on a lonely shore a mistress fair,[23]
Abandoned by a faithless follower
When he grew tired of his illicit love.
Reeling from wine, he bids the fair one stand
Amid the orgies of his wanton band   140
And wear a regal crown upon her head.
Soon Ariadne's fire is added to the stars:[24]
This tribute Liber to his mistress pays
That she should light the heavenly vault above.

The ignorant, foolish rabble in those days   145
Believed all kings had such amazing powers,
That emperors, with all their perfidy,
Could pass to lasting reign in heavenly courts.
Then men believed the royal might and power,

---
18 Cf. *ibid.* 8.270; 7.659.
19 Cf. Ovid, *Fasti* 3.720.
20 Cf. Vergil, *Aeneid* 2.504.
21 Cf. *ibid.* 1.739.
22 Cf. Vergil, *Georgics* 2.380.
23 Cf. Vergil, *Aeneid* 5.613.
24 Cf. Ovid, *Metamorphoses* 8.175-179.

However weak, possessed a strength divine 150
And heavenly right: they even worshiped kings
With shrines and incense, which fear, love, or hope
Increased and fixed as custom for all times,
And this display of spurious piety[25]
The mists of error through the ages spread. 155
Then reverence shown to living kings was paid
To them when they no longer saw the light,
And worship was transferred to their dark urns.
Hence virgins were seduced and children born,
Young men were loved, adulterers were caught 160
Because the courts were wont to be on fire
With royal vices, and offspring of gods,
In their delights, forgot all modesty.

In passing let me touch on your forbears
From heaven, O Rome, Gradivus, Cytherea, 165
Because of whom men claim you half divine;
One violates a priestess, one a mate
From Phrygia weds. The union was unmeet
For both: for wedlock with an earthly lord
Did not become a goddess, nor ravishment 170
Of a maid and furtive love befit a god.
A woman of patrician blood in fact,
Venus espoused a man of vulgar birth;
If Rhea, won by love of wanton Mars,[26]
Gave up her chastity amid the sedge, 175
I would believe some man of noble rank,
But evil character, defiled the maid
And feigned divinity, that none might dare
To blame the wretched girl for his vile deed.
This myth or fraud led our Italian sires 180
To celebrate the rites of Mars at Rome,
To grave upon the Palatine Capitol

---
25 Cf. Vergil, *Aeneid* 6.405.
26 Cf. *ibid.* 7.550; Ovid, *Fasti* 3.11-22.

The names of Grecian Pallas and Jupiter,
To summon Juno from her African height,
Gods kin to Mars; it led their kings to bring   185
Nude Venus from the Erycinian mount,[27]
The mother of the gods from Phrygia,[28]
And from green Naxos Bacchic revelries.[29]
All earth-born deities have found one home,
And you may count as many shrines of gods   190
At Rome as tombs of heroes in the world,
For dead men deified our people venerate.
Such Ancus, Numa, Tullus, Numitor
Considered gods, such fled the Trojan flames,
Such Vesta, the Palladium, household gods,   195
And fear of such the ancient refuge saved.
When superstition entered pagan hearts,
It passed down through a thousand generations
Without a break. The youthful heir adored
All that his hoary sires had shown to be   200
Worthy of veneration. Infants drank
The error with their milk and when they cried
Had tasted sacrificial meal and watched
Wax-coated stones and black gods smeared with oil.
The child had seen a sacred image stand   205
Within the home, Fortune with golden horn,
And his pale mother praying at its feet.
Then lifted by his nurse, he pressed his lips
Upon the stone and poured forth childish prayers,
Asking for riches from a sightless rock,   210
Convinced that what he wished must thence be sought.
He raised not eyes and heart to Wisdom's throne,
But credulous clung to his barren rites,
Honoring his household gods with blood of lambs.
When he went forth on public festal days   215

---
27 Cf. Vergil, *Aeneid* 5.759.
28 Cybele. Cf. Vergil, *Aeneid* 9.80; Minucius Felix, *Octavius* 7.3 (Vol. 10, this series).
29 Cf. Vergil, *Aeneid* 3.125.

And saw the games, the lofty capitol,
The laureled priests before the temples stand,
The Sacred Way, loud with its lowing herds
Before the shrine of Rome (for she receives
Offerings of blood as a divinity   220
And temples of the City and Venus rise
To equal heights and incense burns to both),
He held as true the Senate's high decrees
And put his faith in idols, deeming gods
Of heaven the statues standing in a row.   225
Alcides stands in bronze, Arcadia's guest[30]
When Gades he had spoiled; the brothers twain,
Dishonored Leda's bastard progeny,
Nocturnal horsemen, gods of lofty Rome,
Lean forward on their lance and fix their feet,   230
Heralds of victory, in a lake of lead.[31]
By these the figures stand of ancient kings,
Tros, Italus, and two-faced Janus then,
Father Sabinus, Saturn, Picus stained
By drinking the deadly potion of his bride.[32]   235
A shabby altar is in front of each;
Throngs sacrifice to Janus in his month
With auspices and sacred feasts, and men,
Alas, the old-time kalends still observe
With festal rites. So has the practice grown,   240
Begun in evil times by our forebears
And handed down to sons of later days,
Whose darkened hearts prolonged the vicious chain
And spread the cult to ages without shame.

Clinging to olden rites, these scions adored   245
Augustus with a month, shrine, altar, priest,
Appeased him with a calf and lamb, lay prone

---
30 Cf. *ibid.* 8.51; 201-204.
31 Cf. Cicero, *De natura deorum* 2.6; Minucius Felix, *Octavius* 7.3 (Vol. 10, this series).
32 Cf. Vergil, *Aeneid* 7.177-191.

Before his couch, and oracles conjured.
Inscriptions witness this, and Senate laws
To build to Caesar a shrine like that of Jove.   250
They launched a cult to Livia as Juno.
Her marriage was not less perfidious
Than Saturnia's, who her brother wed.³³
She had not yet brought forth her unborn child,
The son she bore of former spouse conceived,³⁴   255
And couch and marriage bed are both prepared;
The husband calls his friends when her womb stirs,
Sure now of his betrothed's fruitfulness.
The rapturous stepfather will not wait
For his stepson's slow birth, and mid rude chants   260
Another's son to that new lord is born.
The oracles of the gods, Apollo's cave,
This answer gave that never is wedlock
More blest than when the bride is found with child.
This woman thou, O Rome, hast made divine   265
And placed among thy Flora's and Venuses!³⁵
No wonder, for what thinking man but knew
These goddesses were living mortal folk,
Who for their grace of form were so renowned
In amours that they tarnished their fair names.   270

What of Antinous in heaven set,³⁶
That favorite of a prince now deified,
The Ganymede of Hadrian the god
And robbed of manhood in the royal arms,
Not his cupbearer but associate,   275
Who with his Jove drank sacred wine and heard
With his consort the prayers in temples made?

---

33 Juno, daughter of Saturn, who was married to her brother, Jupiter.
34 Cf. Suetonius, *De vita Caesarum* 2.62.
35 Cf. *ibid.* 6.11.
36 Antinous was a Bithynian youth of whom the emperor Hadrian was so fond that he set up statues and images of him at his death and declared that he had been changed into a constellation. Cf. Dio, *Roman History* 69.11.2.

Under such Trajan, Nerva, Severus,
Titus, and valiant Neros waged their wars,
Heroes whom earthly glory signalized,   280
And mortal prowess raised to heights of fame
While cringing under such unhallowed myths!
How shameful that such brave men should believe
The Roman armies could be ruled by Mars,
That vile adulterer who won the Paphian   285
By heaping favors on Aeneas' sons!
How happy they, if they had known the source
Of all their blessings was God, Christ, who willed
That kingdoms run their course, Rome's triumphs grow,
And He Himself should come into the world!   290
But in the shrines of Jove, Augustus, and
The two Junos, of Venus and of Mars,
They sacrificed their darkened, blinded souls
And plunged them deep into the pit of death,
Convinced that the all-ruling dwelt in mire   295
And in the universal depths was sunk.
All marvels of the earth and sea they thought
Were gods. Hills, oceans, rivers, fire, our sires
Embodied for themselves in various shapes,
Inscribing on dumb statues names of men   300
And calling ocean Neptune, river beds
Cyanean Nymphs and forests Dryades,
Or pathless rural glades Nymphs of the dells.
The fire itself, created for our use,
Is titled Vulcan and with power divine   305
Is pictured; like a god in name and face,
He has his shrines and governs furnaces,
Smith of Aeolia or of Etna's vaults.[37]

Some men have sought godhead in shining stars
And dared to deify the sun, on whom   310
Is laid the lot of bearing sleepless toil

---

[37] Cf. Vergil, *Aeneid* 8.416-422.

Along a certain path in sight of men,
Whirled through his orbit as a polished globe
And smaller, none denies, than world and sky.
For larger is the field than one who runs, 315
And wider is the course, on which the wheel
Glows as it turns upon its axle swift.
Though some think that the earth's circumference
Is shorter than that glorious round, and that
The huge star's flames extend beyond a zone 320
Greater than that of earth, yet is the orb
Of heaven smaller and more limited,
Whose surface by a compass, reaching far
From its inner mark, can scarcely be traversed?
He is true God, who all material things 325
Transcends, who has no limits, who over all
Presides, and bounds and fills all things at once.
A fixed zone holds and hedges in the sun,
It shows itself at different times: at morn
It rises, sets at eve, and hides at night, 330
Nor can it turn its torch toward the Wain,
Or move sideways toward the North Wind's gates,
Or turn around and change its wonted course.
Shall this, then, be a god, which must perform
The tasks by law assigned? To man himself 335
A greater freedom has been given, for he
May change his life and mind, whether he choose
To go up by the path on the right or down
The smooth way on the left,[38] to rest or work,
To obey God or turn against His will. 340
This power the Creator has not given
To the sun, which governs the round of days
And as a slave fulfills his destined role.
This star is thought to drive a car and team
And pictured with the rays about his head, 345
His whip and reins and harness and the breasts

---
38 Cf. *ibid.* 6.541-543; Prov. 4.27.

Of panting steeds agleam with ornaments
Of gilded bronze, of marble, or of brass.
After the robes of state, the ivory staff
And curule chair, an old man bends to kiss 350
The feet of bronze, if it can be believed,
And decks with roses or with incense sprays
The moveless wheels and the unbending reins.

This we might bear somehow. But do not shades
Of lowest hell give gods to thee, O Rome? 355
The queen of Furies, Proserpine, the bride
Of Hades' king, from Stygian cave uplifts
Her head, and Romans sacrifice to her
A barren heifer when she visits them.
In heaven and hell she is supposed to reign,[39] 360
And now to drive her oxen team, now force
Her sisters on the world with whips of snakes,[40]
Now shower arrows on the backs of goats,
And though the same, to put on threefold form.[41]
When she is Luna, she shines in splendid robes, 365
When hurling darts, she is Latona's child,
When seated on her throne, Pluto's consort,[42]
Ruling the Furies and fierce Megaera.
If truth you seek, by name of Trivia
A hellish fiend is worshiped, who transports 370
You to the sky and makes you venerate
A star as god, or forces you to stray
Along the world's death-dealing woodland paths
And see a goddess in the groves, who wounds
Men's trembling hearts and slays their reckless souls 375
With mortal blow, then plunges stricken spirits
Beneath the earth so that they pray to gods
Of darkness and submit to powers of night.

---
39 Cf. Vergil, *Aeneid* 6.247.
40 Cf. *ibid.* 6.572.
41 Cf. Claudian, *De raptu Pros.* 1.15.
42 Cf. Vergil, *Aeneid* 1.506.

Behold the criminal offerings made to Dis,[43]
For whom the gladiator is sacrificed 380
To Phlegethon, victim, alas, of Rome!
What means the impious skill of senseless sport,
The slaughter of young men, the pleasure fed
On blood, the circus' mortal strife, and pomp
Of wretched shows in the amphitheatre held?[44] 385
Charon, appeased by pious crime, receives
Due offerings as the guide of victims slain.
These are the joys of the infernal Jove,[45]
In these, the dark Avernian chief finds bliss.
Is it not shameful that a mighty race 390
Should make such offerings for the nation's weal
And seek divine support from caves of hell?
It calls death's ruler from his dark abode
And offers him rich human sacrifice.
Vain is our wonted scorn of Tauric rites:[46] 395
For Latiaris human blood is shed
And throngs make savage offerings at the shrine
Of their Pluto. What holier than the place
Which drinks the blood drawn forth by mystic swords?
Do you doubt that there dwells in nether gloom 400
The god you seek among the silent shades?
Look! Why deny the dead are reckoned gods?
Your fathers' monuments are proof. I read,
'To spirits deified,'[47] on marble tombs
That throng the Latin and Salarian roads. 405
Tell me to whom you grave this line, unless
You honor Orcus as a deity?

---

43 Cf. *ibid.* 12.199.
44 Cf. Claudian, *Panegyricus dictus Manlio Theodoro Consuli* 293.
45 Pluto.
46 Cf. Ovid, *Tristia* 4.4.63; Tertullian, *Apology* 9.5 (Vol. 10, this series); Minucius Felix, *Octavius* 30.4 (Vol. 10, this series).
47 *Dis Manibus.* Sepulchral inscriptions dating from the Augustan age begin with these words. Divine honors were paid to the *dii manes,* or souls of the departed. Cf. Ovid, *Fasti* 2.842; Augustine, *De civitate Dei* 8.26 (Vol. 14, this series).

By such rites from our fathers handed down
The seat of highest empire was defiled,
Until a prince, twice victor over despots,[48]   410
Turned eyes triumphant on her noble walls.
He saw a city, shrouded with black clouds,
Beset with shades of night; and murky air
Shut out the sunlight from her seven hills.
Then moved with pity, he addressed her thus: 415
'O faithful mother, lay aside thy gloom!
For splendid vesture thou art famed, proud spoils
And plenitude of gold adorn thy head,
But flitting vapors stain thy lofty crest,
A lurid light and leaden sky bedim   420
Thy very gems, and smoke that swirls around
Thy face discolors thy bright diadem.
I see dim shadows round thee hovering,
Dark spirits and black idols fly about.
I urge thee, lift thy head above the earth   425
And leave the raging storms beneath thy feet.
The whole world yields to thee; that thou dost rule
The world as mistress and dost plant thy foot
On all things mortal, God Himself has willed.
It is not meet for thee, as queen to mind   430
The things of earth[49] or seek divinity
In lower regions, which thou dost command.
While I am prince, I shall not let thee hold
Old fallacies, nor worship monstrous gods.
If they are stone, they wear away with age   435
Or crumble at a blow; if plaster cased
In metal, faulty cement will relax;
If statues are designed from plates of bronze,[50]
The hollow frames will bend beneath their weight
And fall apart, or scaly rust will eat   440

---

48 Theodosius, who after his defeat of Maximus and Eugenius, suppressed pagan worship.
49 Cf. Col. 3.2.
50 Cf. Arnobius, *Adversus Nationes* 6.16.

Into the figures, piercing them with holes.
Let earth not be thy god, nor star above,
Nor ocean, nor a power that hides below,
Doomed to infernal darkness for its crimes,
Nor yet of human virtues fashion gods, 445
Nor spectral shapes of wandering spirits or souls.
Far be it from thee that a ghost or place,
A genius or a phantom be thy god.
Leave heathen deities to savage tribes,
To whom all fear has made them dread is blest, 450
Whom signs and wonders force to put their faith
In frightful gods, whom bloody feasts delight,
When in a grove they slay the fattened beast
And surfeited with wine, devour its flesh.
It is a shame for thee, who hast imposed 455
Thy laws on conquered tribes and hast refined
Their savage ways of life and war throughout
Thy vast empire, to cling to false beliefs
And superstitions held by brutish folk
In their perverse, unreasoning ignorance. 460
Whether I arm for war, whether I rule
In peace, whether, within the city's walls
I triumph over two usurpers quelled,
Thou must, O queen, acknowledge my ensigns,
On which the cross appears agleam with gems 465
Or borne on lofty shafts in solid gold.
By this sign Constantine was conqueror,[51]
When having crossed the Alps, he broke the chains
Maxentius and his court had forged for thee.
Thou didst then mourn a hundred senators 470
Condemned to death. Or a man who wept
The rape of his betrothed by a wretch
Was plunged in darkness, bound with cruel chains;
Or if a bride, called to the royal bed
Began to satisfy the tyrant's lust, 475

---

[51] Cf. Eusebius, *De vita Constantini* 1.28.

The groom would expiate his ire by death.
The prisons of the cruel prince were filled
With fathers of maidens; if a sire bewailed
His daughter's seizure, he could not betray
His pain or sorrow with impunity.[52] 480
The Mulvian Bridge was witness of the might
That blessed the Christian victor's arms when he
Advanced on Rome and into Tiber's stream
The tyrant hurled, what standard he upbore
What holy sign upon his javelins gleamed. 485
The sign of Christ in gold and gems adorned
The labarum[53] and on the shields was graved;[54]
The cross of Christ shone on the helmets' crests.
The noble senators recall that day
When they marched forth from prison, with their hair 490
All matted and their limbs in fetters bound,[55]
And clinging to the victor's feet in tears,
Lay prone before that glorious sign. That day
The Senate glorified the cross and adored
The name of Christ, borne by avenging troops. 495
Shun after this, O capital of the world,
Thy wonted worship of insensate fiends
And learn the power of the one true God.
Renounce thy childish festivals, thy rites
And cults, unworthy of a realm so great. 500
Cleanse marbles stained with blood, O noble lords!
Let statues, works of famous artists, stand
Unsoiled, our country's fairest ornaments,
And let no shameful use these monuments
Of art defile, or make them cause of sin.' 505

---

[52] The following line is added here in some MSS: *vim libertatis nimiae, patriumque dolorem.*
[53] The standard of Constantine with the letters XP, representing the name of Christ.
[54] Cf. Vergil, *Aeneid* 2.392.
[55] Cf. *ibid.* 2.277.

The city, taught by such edicts, forsook
Her ancient errors and the turbid clouds
Shook from her aged face, her leaders quick,
At their great leader's call, to follow Christ
And place their hope in everlasting life.   510
Then Rome, enlightened in old age, first blushed
For her past centuries, ashamed and grieved
At years gone by with their idolatry.
When she remembered that the soil hard by
Her walls was drenched with martyrs' guiltless blood   515
And saw around her scores of frowning tombs,
She mourned her frightful sentences, her rage
And frenzied sanction of her shameful rites.
She made amends for wounds of righteousness
By late obedience and prayers for grace;   520
Lest her great realm with cruelty be charged
For scorn of justice, she atonement made[56]
And with great love embraced the Christian faith.
Of less worth was the triumph of Marius
When through the cheering throngs he dragged Jugurtha,   525
Nor did the consul from Arpinum bring[57]
So great a boon to thee, O Rome, when he
Doomed Cethegus, as that conferred on thee
In our time by a noble prince, who banned
Many a Catiline, not plotting fires   530
For thy abodes, nor steel for senators,
But darkest hell and torments for men's souls.
Fiends wandered through the temples and through courts,
They held the Forum and the Capitol,[58]
They had set snares to capture people's hearts   535
And in their very marrow they instilled
A secret poison that spread through their souls.
A peaceful conqueror of hidden foes,

---

56 Cf. *ibid.* 4.636.
57 Cicero, who was born at Arpinum.
58 Cf. Vergil, *Aeneid* 8.361,653.

That prince gained bloodless victories and led
The land of Quirinus to realms above.   540
No bounds he set, no limits fixed of time;
An empire without end he showed,[59] lest power
And glory won by Rome should ever wane.

One could see senators, lights of the world,
And throngs of old Catos exult to wear,   545
With whiter toga, snowy robes of faith
And put aside their priestly ornaments.
The Evandrian Senate,[60] sons of Annius
And children of the Probi,[61] with but few
Left on Tarpeia's rock, hasten to shrines   550
Of Nazarenes and apostolic fonts.
First to adorn the city's head, they say,
Was great Anicius (Rome, herself, thus boasts);
Heir of the blood and name of Olybrius
And consul in the palm emblazoned robe,   555
He lowered Brutus' rods at martyrs' shrines
And in Christ's honor bent the Ausonian ax.
Paulinus and Bassus gave themselves to Christ[62]
With lively faith and lifted up the scions
Of a patrician house to future bliss.   560
Why in my verses tell how the Gracchi,
Friends of the people, sure in power and rank,
Gave orders for the statues of the gods
To be thrown down[63] and with their lictors vowed
Themselves to Christ and His all-powerful rule?   565
We may count hundreds of old families[64]

---

59 Cf. *ibid.* 1.288-289.
60 Evander, the founder of a city on the site of Rome, is credited with establishing the Senate.
61 Cf. Claudian, *Probino et Olybrio* 143. The Christian family of the Anicii Probi was renowned for its wealth and prominence in the government of Rome. Cf. Vol. 16, this series, pp. 268-273.
62 St. Paulinus of Nola, bishop and poet (357-431); Junius Bassus, Prefect of Rome in 358, was the first of his family to become a Christian.
63 Cf. Jerome, *Ep.* 107.3.
64 Cf. Statius, *Thebaid* 3.600.

Of noble blood, who to Christ's standard turned
And raised themselves from depths of paganism.
If any image of the city exists,
It is in these; if great men represent   570
The nation's character, all these do so
When joined by good men of one mind with them.
Mark the grand hall where meet the civic lights:
You will find few still bound by pagan folly
And barely clinging to abolished cults,   575
Who would preserve the darkness of the past,
Or spurn the splendor of the noonday sun.

Now to the people turn your eyes. How few
Who do not scorn Jove's altar stained with blood!
The common crowd who to their attics climb,   580
Who wear out pavements walking to and fro[65]
And fare on bread doled out from lofty steps,
Now seek the tomb on Vatican hill, where lie
The ashes, pledge of their great Father's love,[66]
Or hasten to the Lateran to receive   585
The King's anointing with the sacred sign.[67]
Do we still doubt that Rome to Thee, O Christ,
Has given herself and yielded to Thy laws,
And that with all her people and great men
She now extends her realm beyond the stars?   590
I am not moved when some men keep their eyes
Closed in the light of day and go astray.
Though famed for merit and for noble blood,
Though heaped with laurels and titles of renown,
Though they are listed in the calendar   595
And mark the yearly record with their names,

---

65 Cf. Juvenal 6.350.
66 St. Peter. Cf. *Peristephonon* 12.29-31 (Vol. 43, this series).
67 Baptism. The great Lateran palace, belonging to the family of the Laterani from early times, was given to the Church by Constantine about the year 313. A basilica, now St. John Lateran, with a baptistery attached, was constructed in connection with the palace under the direction of Constantine.

Though with the ancients found in wax or bronze,
These few, now without following, do not
Make up the senate or represent the state.
The views they foster, only some endorse, 600
And now infrequently; the nation's will
Opposes and condemns their timid plaints.
If laws of conscript fathers in ancient times
Were valid only when the records showed
Three hundred senators had sanctioned them, 605
Let us maintain this rule; and let the voice
Of the minority in silence yield.

See how our benches in the senate rule
That Jove's vile couch and all idolatry
Be banished from our city's noble walls. 610
Great numbers to that section freely cross
To which our worthy emperor's voice leads.
No place is there for spite, no one is forced;
That all will thus is clear; they are convinced
And follow, not commands, but reason's choice. 615
Our generous prince, rewarding all alike,
Confers on pagans highest dignities
And lets them seek the homage of their own,
Nor hinders men still sunk in idol cults
From reaching earthly heights, for things divine 620
Debar men not from life in wonted ways.
He named thee[67] to the consulship and seat
Of judgment, gave the toga trimmed with gold,
He whose belief offends thee, champion
Of dying gods, thou who alone dost plead 625
For the return of Vulcan's wiles and tricks
Of Mars and Venus, Saturn's stones and rage
Of Phoebus, the Ilian mother's festival,[69]
The rites of Nysian Bacchus, Isis' mimes

---

68 Symmachus.
69 Cybele. Cf. Ovid, *Fasti* 4. 181-186.

For lost Osiris, sport of her bald heads,[70]
And all the phantoms of the Capitol.

O speech that wells from wondrous fount of words,
The crown of Roman eloquence that vies
With Tullius himself! What gems flow forth
From that rich source! Lips worthy to be dyed
In everlasting gold had they praised God,
But they were stained with laud of monstrous fiends!
It was as if a man should try to turn
The sod with rakes of ivory, or till
The ground with fork of gold; the muddy soil
Would dim the brightness of the burnished prongs
And smear the precious tool with squalid earth.

I fear no charge of rashness, nor that men
May think I enter on a clash of wits;
I know myself and my poor gifts too well.
Rude as I am in speech, I would not dare
To challenge arrows darted by that tongue.
Let his book be untouched, and his great work
Hold fast the fame won by its eloquence.
But let me save my breast from wounds and turn
Aside the flying javelins with my shield.
For if our faith, safe in this age of peace,
Has been assailed by crafty, warlike foes,
Why should I not ward off their airy shafts,
So that their wasted blows may be in vain?

But it is time to halt the march of this small book
Lest my unbroken song may cause offense.

---

[70] Cf. Minucius Felix, *Octavius* 23.1 (Vol. 10, this series).

AGAINST SYMMACHUS

(CONTRA SYMMACHUM)

Book Two

AGAINST SYMMACHUS

Book Two

Preface

Simon, who was surnamed Peter,[1]
Chief disciple of Christ the Lord,
On a day at the set of sun
When the evening sky grows red,
Had unloosened his anchor's hook,   5
Filled the sails with the swelling winds,
And made ready to cross the sea.
But night roused a contrary gale[2]
That stirred up the deep-seated waves
And buffeted the floundering boat.   10
Shouts of mariners struck the sky,
With their shrieks and despairing groans
Amid creaking of swaying ropes,
Nor did any have hope of escape
From shipwreck and a watery death,   15
When the oarsmen all wan with fear
Saw Christ himself not far away
Treading surely upon the surge,
Just as though on the barren shore
He walked over the solid ground.   20
All the rest of the sailors stood
Affrighted at this miracle;
Peter only without alarm

---
1 Cf. Acts 10.5; Matt. 10.2.
2 Cf. Matt. 14.24-32; Mark 6.45-51; John 6.16-21.

Knew the Lord of the heavenly throne,
Of the earth and the pathless sea, 25
Whose omnipotent power subdues
Restless waters beneath His feet.
He raised suppliant hands in prayer
And entreated the well-known help,
But Christ, nodding assuringly, 30
Bade him leap from the tossing ship.
Straightway Peter obeyed the word,
But scarcely had he wet his soles
On the crest of the foaming waves
When his tottering steps gave way 35
And his feet were about to sink.
God upbraided this mortal man
For his lack of a steadfast faith
And the strength to surmount the flood
As a follower of Christ the Lord. 40
Then his servant He lifted up
And held him and taught him to walk
On the waves of the swollen sea.

Thus I by my loquacious tongue
From the haven of silence am led 45
Into perils unknown and dark,
Not as Peter, disciple true,
Confident in his virtue and faith,
But as one whom unnumbered sins
Have shipwrecked on the rolling seas. 50
Bold I am, it is true indeed,
When with consciousness of the night
I am passing in my dark life,
I fear not to expose my bark
To the waves of so great a man,[3] 55
Than whom none is more skilled today.
In the storms of his eloquence

---
[3] Symmachus.

He leaps, thunders and roars and swells.
He can easily shipwreck me,
One untaught in seafaring arts, 60
Unless Thou, O Almighty Christ,
Stretch Thy hand forth with help divine,
That the blast of his powerful words
May not plunge me into the flood,
But, advancing with careful steps, 65
I may walk on the surging waves.

Thus far the subject of my song has been
The birth of gods of old, the origin
Of pagan cults and Rome's belief in Christ.
Now I shall face my foe and make reply.[4]
Whence say they he began that he might bend 5
The hearts of our good lords[5] with suasive arts?
These militant chieftains in the flower of youth,[6]
Born in their father's wars, reared in the mold
Of their grandsire, fired by ancestral fame,
This clever orator sways, as if war-trumps 10
He blared, and stirs their spirits with words like these:
'If victory won and to be won, my lords,
Is dear to you, let the chaste goddess keep
Her shrine while you now reign. Is any man
Such friend to foes as to grudge her worship 15
In your empire, which she so glorifies?'[7]

The princes calmly answered the envoy's words:
'We know how sweet is victory to the brave,
Most fluent speaker of the Latin tongue,

---

[4] Cf. Vergil, *Georgics* 1-2.
[5] Honorius and Arcadius, the youthful sons of Theodosius, who became co-emperors of the East and West at the death of their father in 395.
[6] Cf. Vergil, *Aeneid* 8.160.
[7] Cf. Symmachus, *Relatio* 3.

But we know in what way she must be sought; 20
As boys our father trained us in this art
And when a boy he learned it from his sire.
Altars and meal do not bring victory:[8]
Unending toil, stout courage, lofty spirit,
Zeal, vigor, and precaution, all of these 25
Bring victory, when joined with force of arms.[9]
If warriors lack these, though a Victory
Of golden talents made, unfold bright wings
In a marble shrine, she will not stand by them
And by reverses manifest offense. 30
O soldier, doubtful of your own main force,
Why from a woman's statue seek support?
No armed cohort has seen a maid with wings
Guiding the darts of panting warriors.
Seek you the cause of victory? It is 35
The hand of man and God's almighty power,
No warlike woman with her hair caught up,
Feet bare, and bosom girt with flowing scarf.
The painter's brush has taught you to create[10]
A god from monsters by the poets feigned, 40
Or from your shrines the artist has derived
A figure he has matched in liquid wax,
And aided by the flights of poetry,
Has archly painted it with colored dyes.
Thus these one path pursue, thus empty dreams 45
Homer, Apelles, Numa, all conceive,
And painting, poetry, and idolatry
Thrive on their triple motive of deceit.
If this is not so, why do poets' tales
Inspire frescoes and waxen images? 50
Why does the priest of Phrygia maim himself
When poetry fair Attis has unmanned?

---

8 Cf. Ambrose, *Epist.* 18.7 (Vol. 26, this series).
9 Claudian, *De tertio cons. Hon.* 144.
10 Cf. Wisd. 15.4,5.

Why are hoofed horses kept from Trivia's shrine[11]
And sacred woodlands, when the Muse has dragged
A virtuous youth and chariot on the shore   55
And a wall displays the scene in many hues?
If you have any shame, idolater,
Cease giving fancied shapes to spiritual things,
Cease covering human backs with down: in vain
You call a woman goddess and bird of prey.   60
Would you, O Rome, adorn your Senate house?
Hang there the trophies won by blood and arms,
Gather the diadems of conquered kings,
But break the sordid idols you have banned;
Then in your hall the memory will be kept   65
Of victory not of earth but beyond the stars.'

When with such words our princes have replied,
He goes on and his deep-toned trumpet sounds;
He mentions ancient custom and contends
That wonted ways are dear, and states and men   70
Have their own laws. 'As children are at birth
Endowed with varied souls,' he says, 'likewise
Each city, when its walls first rise, receives
A genius which directs its destiny.'[12]
He adds that hidden truths and mysteries   75
Can be sensed through good fortune that gives proof
Of blessing, if that which men undertake
Turns out well; that for our forbears the cult
Of idols ever brought prosperity.
He cites the glorious past and pictures Rome,   80
Grown old, with snow-white hair and wrinkled brow,
Pleading that her divinities be restored:
'I am free, let me live in my own way.
Will any blame me for my thousand years?
All dwell beneath the sun and breathe one air,   85

---
11 Cf. Vergil, *Aeneid* 7.778-780.
12 Cf. Symmachus, *Relatio* 8; Vergil, *Aeneid* 1.437.

All living creatures share one atmosphere,
But who and what God is, by divers paths
We seek, and over roadways far apart
We reach the selfsame Being: each race draws near
This mystery in its accustomed way.'[13]   90
To these words uttered with such eloquence
Faith has replied, for she alone unlocks
The mysteries of orthodox belief.
For when we treat of things divine and strive
To know that One who no beginning had,   95
Nor will have end, who prior to chaos was
And made the universe, our human mind
Is too finite and weak for this great task.[14]
If our weak nature tries to penetrate,
With gaze too keen, the mysteries of God,   100
Who can doubt that the feeble sight will fail,
That weary mental powers will be confused
And sink beneath the weight of futile toil.
The easy way of faith leads to belief
In an Almighty Father who bestows   105
His blessings on us now and promises
Eternal joys, so that we perish not
Nor vanish wholly after this brief life.
Discern the Giver through the gift itself:
From God are gifts eternal and divine,   110
The gifts of men are passing and short-lived.
All temporal things are transient and cheap,
Unworthy of an everlasting Giver,
Who has the fullness of being without end
And gives to man that which will never end.   115
For if God gives us perishable gifts
And nought more precious has, then He is poor
And weak, unworthy of the highest praise,
Not infinite, but mere shadow of godhead.

---
13 Cf. Symmachus, *ibid.* 9 and 10.
14 Cf. Prov. 25.27; Sir. (Ecclus.) 3.22.

Faith argues thus, nay even has no doubt 120
That one true God exists, who bids us hope
Our life and being will not see lasting death
If we are worthy. 'If you would,' He says,
'Ascend to heaven, banish cares of earth.
For far as earth is distant from the sky 125
And heaven from the world below, so far
Are your vain thoughts from my eternal thoughts,[15]
Ill from good, sin from virtue, dark from light.
I counsel you to shun all passing things
And deem as nought all to corruption prone, 130
For it is destined to return to nought.
All earth brings forth and holds, at dawn of time
I made; I decked with splendid ornaments
The shining world and formed the elements,
But willed that their enjoyment be confined 135
Within due bounds, as far as mortal frame
And fleeting human life may have the need,
Not that man, by unbridled passion ruled,
Should reckon good alone things sweet and vain,
Which I have preordained to pass with time. 140
The span of life I fixed to prove men's souls,
Lest virtue never tried might lack the strength
For winning glory on the wrestling field.
Seductive and pernicious is the taste
Of passing things that captivate the heart[16] 145
And hold it fast. Indulgence must be curbed,
And from its snares the soul must be set free,
Lest soft, tenacious fetters weigh it down.
Man must strive lustily and virtue's path
Must tread, and he must not find his delight 150
In temporal things, amass great stocks of gold,[17]
Turn avid gaze on many-colored gems,

---
15 Cf. Isa. 55.9.
16 Cf. Lactantius, *Div. inst.* 6.22.5 (Vol. 49, this series).
17 Cf. Tibullus 1.1.1.

Show off to gain the favor of the crowd[18]
And swell with pride at worldly fame, extend
His heritage of patrimonial lands 155
And set his heart upon a neighbor's fields,[19]
Indulge the flesh in all he wills and does,
Prefer material gain to righteousness;[20]
But place all hope in Me, that what I give
Will never fade and will forever last.' 160

When God this promise makes, what noble spirit
In preference to eternal gifts would choose
Ephemeral things? What sober man would rate
The joys of sense above the soul's rewards?
What sets a man apart from brutes if not 165
That beasts see present goods, while I have hope
Of goods beyond all time and human sight?
For if my life will perish with my flesh
And all I am cannot last after death,[21]
What heavenly king, what maker of the world, 170
What god or power have I a cause to fear?
Aflame with lust, foul orgies I will taste,
Stain marriage beds, scorn sacred modesty,
Deny a kinsman's unattested trust,[22]
Despoil poor clients greedily, resort 175
To sorcery to end a mother's life,
(By living longer she defrauds the heirs),
And fear no punishment: the laws are spurned,
Justice stands armed, but knows not of the crime,[23]
Or if it knows, the judge is bribed with gold. 180
The ax but rarely strikes the guilty wretch.[24]
But why these thoughts? God with stern majesty

---
18 Cf. Vergil, *Aeneid* 6.816.
19 Cf. Horace, *Satires* 2.6.8.
20 Cf. Horace, *Odes* 4.9.41.
21 Cf. 1 Cor. 15.32; Lactantius, *op. cit.* 3.17.36 (Vol. 49, this series).
22 Cf. Juvenal 13.60.
23 Cf. Tertullian, *Apology* 45.5 (Vol. 10, this series).
24 Cf. Cyprian, *Ad Donatus* 10 (Vol. 36, this series).

Chides me and warns that death will not efface
The record of my deeds: 'The spirit of man
Will never die,' He says; 'it will atone   185
Forever for the body's misconduct.²⁵
To plunge a spiritual being into flames
Is nought for Me. Though it outstrip the wind,
My punishments will overtake the soul,
For I am spirit, Creator of all spirits.   190
Like penalty I shall make the body share,
For to their old-time shape I can restore
The ashes, nor do I resign this power:
The form I made I can raise from the dead.²⁶
Types of my power lie in the seeds themselves:²⁷   195
Nature equips them all to come to life
After their death. For they become dried up
When vital force departs; then dry and dead,
They lie in trench or furrow, buried there,
Until they sprout and from their tombs arise.   200
Can you divine or know what artisan
Arranges this, what virtue acts within?
Poor wretch, be not deceived by scientists!
Creation's Lord, I can restore all things
That have decayed or died and clothe again   205
The withered branch with former flower or leaf:
And I shall do the same one day for man,
Raise him from lifeless ashes and build up
His pristine frame to expiate his sins
In torments or to shine on thrones above,   210
Never again to die in either state.
But while the twofold substance still is one
Let it be mindful of its Author and let
It humbly worship Him.²⁸ The living soul

---

25 Cf. Tertullian, *op. cit.* 45.7 (Vol. 10, this series).
26 Cf. Minucius Felix, *Octavius* 34.9 (Vol. 10, this series).
27 Cf. 1 Cor. 15.36: John 12.24; Minucius Felix, *op. cit.* 34.11 (Vol. 10, this series).
28 Cf. Claudian, *De cons. Stil.* 2.71-72.

Was not by one God made and human frame 215
By one diverse, nor are life's blessings ruled
By many powers; one God does not supply
The crops and ears of wheat, another give
The wine from grapes and make the red juice flow.
I am one God, who fills the olive trees 220
With fruits you deem by Grecian Pallas given,[29]
Who grants Lucina's hours to men at birth.
United by my law in bonds of love,
The sexes joyfully propagate their kind;
By sinful amours you profane this love 225
And under Venus' shadow hide your shame.
Alone I rule the elements, nor tire,
As some weak mortal, from the heavy toil.
Infinite light is mine, eternal life,
And age your human mind can never grasp. 230
I need no help in governing the world,
I seek not partners nor associates.
The hosts of angels fashioned by my hand,
I know what their created nature is
And for what purpose I have destined them. 235
Ignoring Me, you feign a thousand gods
Endowed with my omnipotence, and thus
Make of Me many parts, from whom no part
Can be divorced, for simple entity
Cannot have parts. Composite being alone 240
Can be divided; none created Me,
So I, one God, am not divisible.[30]
I am no part of what I made from nought.
Wherefore, O man, one temple build to Me
And worship Me as one true God. I scorn 245
Your stones, rock hewn from Paros and Punic cliffs,
And Synna, mottled green, from Sparta brought;
Let no man offer Me red stone from crags.

---
29 Cf. Vergil, *Georgics* 2.181.
30 Cf. Lactantius, *op. cit.* 1.3.9 (Vol. 49, this series).

A temple not of stone but of the heart[31]
I love; on gold foundations of faith it rests, 250
Its walls with virtue shine, and justice gilds
The lofty roof, while chastity bestrews
The floor with flowers and guards the entrance hall.
This house is meet for Me, this fair abode
I enter, worthy of its heavenly guest. 255
This dwelling is not new; my glory flowed
Into the flesh, the very light of God
Enlightened man, and for Himself God made
The human body His own resting place.
I had made man a perfect being, had 260
Commanded him to stand upright with eyes[32]
On heaven and his thoughts all turned on Me;
But looking down, he stooped to earthly gain
And from his heart thrust my divinity.
He had to be redeemed: my Spirit came down[33] 265
And impregnated flesh made from the dust
With the divine nature; God has assumed
Humanity, joining it with divinity,
And kindled in men's hearts new love of Me.'

Tell me, most learned judge of Italy, 270
What welcome your ears give to God's precepts.
Without due thought do you cling to old ways,
And does a wise man's keen insight allow
Such words as these: 'Old custom I prefer
To virtue's path, the worship revealed by heaven, 275
Belief in truth and doctrines of the faith'?[34]
If we must hold in reverence and observe
The barbarous customs of the primitive world,

---
[31] Cf. 1 Cor. 3.16; Cyprian, *De idolorum vanitate* 9 (Vol. 36, this series).
[32] Cf. Ovid, *Metamorphoses* 1.84; Lactantius, *op. cit.* 2.1.14 (Vol. 49, this series).
[33] Cf. Luke 1.35.
[34] Cf. Symmachus, *Relatio* 8.

Let us retrace the ages to time's dawn[35]
And choose to scoff at all the usages 280
That were discovered in ensuing years.
When earth was new, no yeomen tilled the fields:[36]
What use the plow or harrow's needless toil?
Better to feed on acorns from the oak.
Men first with wedges split their kindling wood:[37] 285
Let fiery furnaces our axes melt
And let the molten ore flow back to mines.
Slain cattle furnished clothing and frigid caves[38]
The meager homes: let us go back to caverns
And put on hairy garb of unsewn skins. 290
Men, once barbarians, tamed their savage hearts
And grew humane: let them go back again
To their wild shouts and bestial ways of life.
Now let a youth with Scythian duty hurl
His sire from the sacred bridge (such was the rule), 295
Let Saturn's temples smoke with infant deaths[39]
And cruel altars sound with tearful cries.
Let Romans build their huts of fragile straw,[40]
Such as where Remus dwelt, spread royal beds
With hay and on their hairy bodies drape 300
A cloak made from the skin of a Libyan bear.[41]
Such the Sicilian and Tuscan chiefs once wore.
In course of time the Rome of ancient years
Has changed her cults, her dress, her laws and arms.[42]
She worships gods not known when Quirinus reigned; 305
Some things she has improved, some given up,
But has not ceased to change her usages
Or to reverse laws sanctioned long ago.

---
[35] Cf. Vergil, *Georgics* 2.402.
[36] Cf. *ibid.* 1.125.
[37] Cf. *ibid.* 1.144.
[38] Cf. Juvenal 6.2.
[39] Cf. Tertullian, *op. cit.* 9.2-4 (Vol. 10, this series).
[40] Cf. Vergil, *Aeneid* 8.354.
[41] Cf. *ibid.* 5.57; 8.368.
[42] Cf. Tertullian, *op. cit.* 6.9 (Vol. 10, this series).

Why do you cite against me wonted rites,
O Roman Senator, when a change of mind   310
Has made Senate and people alter codes?
Now when it profits us to lay aside
The manners of the past for newer ways,
We take delight in the discovery
Of things not known before; the life of man   315
Grows and improves by long experience.⁴³
Such changes may be seen in human life,
Which varies with each age: the infant crawls,
The boy totters both in step and mind,
The robust youth with fiery passion burns,   320
Then comes the time of ripe maturity,
And last old age, sagacious but infirm,
In body falters, but is sound in mind.
These are the steps through which the human race
Has run its varied course: thus rude at first   325
And sunk in mire, it led a bestial life,
Dragging its infant body on all fours.⁴⁴
Then as a youth, apt in acquiring skills,
It was refined through training in new roles;
Next through the years of passion it evolved,   330
Swollen with vice, until its powers matured;⁴⁵
Now comes the time for tasting things divine
With mind serene, and searching earnestly
Into salvation's hidden mysteries.
Yet if you have such love of age-old ways   335
And shrink from giving up your former rites,
In ancient books a noble instance shows
That at the time of the flood, or long before,
The race then dwelling on the new-formed earth
And in an empty world adored one God.⁴⁶   340

---
43 Cf. Juvenal 13.18.
44 Bergman regards this line, which appears in some MSS, as an interpolation.
45 Cf. Vergil, *Aeneid* 2.639.
46 Cf. Vergil, *Georgics* 1.62.

From it is drawn the long line of our stock,
Which now restores its native piety.
But since we speak of Roman rites, I prove
That Hector's progeny for many years
Invoked not many gods, but were content   345
With scattered shrines and altars on the hills.
Rome came by countless gods, when through her arms
She conquered cities and great triumphs won;
With her victorious hand she gathered up
The idols of the foe from smoking shrines   350
And brought them home as hallowed deities.[47]
One image she from ruins of Corinth snatched,
One she from burning Athens took as prey,
Cleopatra's fall gave statues with dogs' heads,
And having conquered Ammon's sands, she had   355
Among her Afric trophies some with horns.
When Rome acclaimed a conquering general's car,
She added altars of the gods and made
From captured plunder new divinities,
Gods rooted up along with native walls   360
And powerless to protect their sacred shrines.
Do you not see how ancient customs change
And waver in their course from age to age,
Adopting gods not to our fathers known
And making use of strange religious rites[48]   365
Instead of native worship. Every cult
Has come an exile to our hostile shores.
In vain, O bigot, you uphold old rites;
You cherish not ancestral custom, wretch.

Our orator declares that fate assigns   370
A genius to each city by which it lives.
'For every race or city has,' he says,
'A fate or genius like the distinctive souls

---

[47] Cf. Ambrose, *Epist.* 18.30 (Vol. 26, this series).
[48] Cf. Tertullian, *op. cit.* 6.10 (Vol. 10, this series).

That into our new bodies are infused.'⁴⁹
First, what this genius is, I do not know, 375
Or what its nature, powers, or origin,
Whether pure spirit or matter of some kind,
What are its thoughts, what functions it performs.
I know, however, that the souls of men
Spread through the living veins, so that the blood 380
Receives from them its motion and its heat,
And flowing through the members, warms the cold,
Moistens the arid, and the rigid bends.
The living spirit thus rules the life of man,
But you compare it with a fancied genius 385
Of walls, which not now is, nor ever was.
The spirit to the body turns its thought,
Takes care that it is clothed and has support⁵⁰
In weakness, that it shuns appalling fears,
Foresees the useful, learns the various arts, 390
Consults what Master it shall serve and deem
Creator of the world and Lord of all.
But tell me when this genius of the city,
Of which you speak, first entered newborn Rome.
Did it flow from the udders of the wolf 395
And at its birth feed twins in the wooded glen?
Or with the vultures flying through the air,
Did it draw sudden being from a cloud?
Does it rest on the roofs or in the courts?
Does it establish rules and public laws, 400
Or does it enter battlefields, call men to arms
With trumpet sound and hurl them at the foe?
Would this not merit the laughter of the wise?
Let us suppose there is a shade or spirit
That guides the destiny of the commonwealth 405
And is its vital force, why does the state
Not to religious worship give more thought,

---
49 Cf. Symmachus, *Relatio* 8.
50 Cf. Horace, *Epist.* 2.1.136.

Why does it not to heaven freely look,
Why does it as a captive think its fate
Is immutable and bound by natal stars, 410
For now it can refuse what once it chose,
Give up its errors and reform its faith?
For seven hundred years it wandered round,
Not sure what form of government it desired,
Or what regime would rule with equity. 415
Kings ruled the city in the early days,
With elders sharing in authority;
Soon nobles of high rank were at the helm;
Plebeian multitudes with equal rights
Then joined the senators and governed long, 420
Guiding the state in times of war and peace.
The consul spoke for lords, tribune for mob.
This regime soon grew odious and ten men
Were chosen from the nobles, each of whom
Was hedged round with twelve fasces and an ax. 425
Once more two leaders ruled the commonwealth,
And consuls formed the annual registers;
An armed triumvirate stained the final age.
The nation's fate or genius or spirit passed
Through such rude storms; right rule it learned at last, 430
And on Augustus' head it placed a crown,
Naming him father of his country, guide
Of people and senate, leader in warfare,
Dictator and just judge, guardian of wealth,
Avenger of crime, conferrer of dignities.[51] 435
If through so many steps and varied schemes
It formed a regime that commands respect
And public loyalty, why does it fear
To recognize divine authority,
Unknown before and only now revealed? 440
Let us rejoice, for Rome, now thrall to Christ,
Serves one true God and hates her former cults.

---

51 Cf. Claudian, *De quarto cons. Hon.* 118.

Rome's men, I mean, in whom her soul resides,
And not an airy genius you have feigned.
Why do you say that Rome one genius has, 445
When you assign a genius to gates, to homes,
To baths and taverns, and in every place
Imagine thousands of these geniuses,
So that no corner is without its shade?
It follows that a fate may be imposed 450
On every building and each wall will rise
Under its proper star, which will decide
The time of its duration and its fall.
Men grant to stones Lachesis' flimsy threads,
They think the wood depends upon her wheel 455
And to the beams attribute her decrees,
As if it mattered under what star the tree
To be uplifted to the roof was felled.
They say there is no human enterprise,
No earthly event, but has its destined lot. 460
Since they think thus, let them explain why laws
Were on Twelve Tables graved, or why precepts
Threaten wrongdoers, if an iron fate
Drives them by force to unavoidable crime.
By vile suggestions it constrains their will, 465
So that they have no power to resist.
Away, harsh laws, if you have any shame,
Blunt your keen sword that smites the innocent,
Unlock your prisons where you hold a crowd
Of blameless men, for fate has done the wrong! 470
No man has guilt if fate rules life and deeds.[52]
The guilty man is he who freely dares
To sin, for he can choose the right or wrong,
And fate is not to blame, but man incurs
Through his free will both guilt and punishment, 475
Which is his due and is not caused by fate.
Let him who trusts in fate learn that the stars

---
[52] Cf. Seneca, *Oedipus* 1019.

Prevent no man from recognizing God,
That astral law does not spurn piety.
The soul seeks higher things above the stars, 480
It moves beyond the cloudy ways of fate
And tramples under foot the false belief
That at the time of birth its lot is fixed.
Come hither, all mankind and cities, too,
A great light calls you; learn to know your Lord! 485
Free faith lies here, and fate is nought, or if
It does exist, it flees before Christ's face.

But Rome has won success through many gods;[53]
She worships them for triumphs granted her.
Come, warrior, say who gave you Africa 490
And Europe; tell the names of all these gods.
The boon of Jupiter gave you rule of Crete,[54]
Pallas gave Argos; Cynthius, Delphi;
Isis gave Egypt; Venus, the Rhodians;
The huntress maid gave Ephesus; and Mars, 495
The Hebrus; Bromius, Thebes; Juno allowed
Her Africans to serve a Phrygian race,
And that fair city, which 'she fondly aimed,
Did but the fates permit,'[55] to make the head
Of subject tribes, she bade live under Rome. 500
Did all these fall through treachery of their gods,
Do altars lie in ruins through their intrigues?
O loyalty, O sacred faith! These gods
Have left their native lands and trust is placed
In deities that earned respect through flight! 505
Or did the gods attempt to save their people
And strive to rout the hostile Roman troops,
But did the greater prowess of the foe

---

[53] Cf. Symmachus, *Relatio* 9; Ambrose, *Epist.* 18.7 (Vol. 26, this series); Tertullian, *op. cit.* 25.2 (Vol. 10, this series); Minucius Felix, *op. cit.* 25.1 (Vol. 10, this series).
[54] Cf. Cyprian, *De idolorum vanitate* 4.
[55] Vergil, *Aeneid* 1.17-18; Tertullian, *op. cit.* 25.8 (Vol. 10, this series).

Dash them to pieces on the dusty field?
Yes, it is true, false paganism was crushed 510
By force of arms, and glory fled from it.
For people born to war it was not hard
To break such flimsy forces and to bend
The yielding necks of gods of every kind.⁵⁶
Was that a war rude Samnites and Marsians waged 515
Against the weak Dictean Corybantes?
Did the Etruscan soldiers fight with guards
Or athletes smeared with oil for boxing games?
And Mercury with his headgear could not save
His wrestling-schools when Lacedaemon fell. 520
How could Cybeleian troops by eunuch led
Withstand footsoldiers of the Appennines
And all of Asia and Ida's mount defend?
Maybe it was a hard, laborious task
To rout Idalian roses, lyric bard, 525
The bow and quiver of the woodland maid,
And to tread under foot their conquered rites.
On Actium's flood pipes gave the battle sign⁵⁷
To Egypt, trumpets to opposing ranks.
Frail skiffs and shallops forced their Memphian beaks 530
Amid the towering ships, but powerless
Were Serapis and barking Anubis.⁵⁸
The mighty army triumphed, led by chief
Of Julian line from snowy Algidus.
No Venus armed, no mailed Minerva helped, 535
No line of faithless gods exiled from home
Stood by the hardy Roman warriors;
Vanquished before, they did not aid our foes,
If they maintained their old hostility.
You say gods favored nations where their shrines 540
Were always blessed by throngs of worshipers,

---
56 Cf. Vergil, *Aeneid* 8.698.
57 Cf. *ibid.* 8.675-713.
58 Cf. *ibid.* 8.698.

And that the standards of Aeneas' stock
They followed for the love of royal Numa.
When her own fortress fell, did Pallas seek[59]
The tents of Diomede and Ulysses' camp, 545
Where grief bedewed her statue with a sweat?[60]
Or when the Macedonian chief piled high
The smoldering shrines of conquered Amyclae,
Did captured gods choose to be mixed with spoils
And carried to Assyrian Babylon? 550
I cannot bear to slight the name of Rome,
Her hard-fought wars and trophies won by blood.
He who ascribes to Venus Rome's great deeds
Scorns her unconquered arms and prizes gained
And robs her of the palm of victory. 555
In vain we hail great generals in their cars
Placed on the top of a triumphal arch,
Fabricius, Curius, Drusus, or Camillus,[61]
And under foot the captives on bent knee,
Bowed to the yoke, hands tied behind their backs, 560
Their broken darts hung on a laden tree,
If Flora, Matuta, Ceres, or Laurentina
Crushed Brennus, Antiochus, Perses, Pyrrhus,
And Mithridates, 'and through their auspices
The bird of fortune brought us victory.' 565
If Apollo's crow with wing or beak gave aid
To Corvinus, what is valor or renown?
Why did that crow ignore the tragic day
When corpses covered Cannae's luckless field[62]
And the consul perished on a heap of dead? 570
Why on the Cremera's banks did no god warn
Three hundred Fabii would in battle fall
And leave scarce one survivor of their race?[63]

---
[59] Cf. *ibid.* 2.166.
[60] Cf. *ibid.* 2.173-174.
[61] Cf. Juvenal 8.3.
[62] Cf. Claudian, *De bello Gothico* 387.
[63] Cf. Ovid, *Fasti* 195-242.

Did no Tritonian owl to Carrhae fly
Advising Crassus of the goddess' help,   575
Or did no snowy doves the Paphian bring[64]
To scare the Persian race with her bright zone?

I see what moves you in these instances
Of ancient gallantry: you say the world
On land and sea was conquered, you retrace[65]   580
The thousands of triumphant victories
And heavy spoils borne through the midst of Rome.
Would you, O Roman, have me tell the cause
Of your success and of the high renown
That has imposed your yoke upon the world?   585
God willed to join the peoples and the realms
Of different languages and hostile cults[66]
Under the same empire and make all men
Accept the bonds of one harmonious rule,
So that religion might unite all hearts;   590
For there can be no union worthy of Christ
Unless one spirit reigns throughout the earth.
Concord alone knows God, alone it pays
Due homage to the Father: harmony
Among men wins His blessings for the world,   595
Discord drives Him away, war saddens Him,
Peace pleases Him, good will possesses Him.
In all lands bounded by the western sea
And brightened by Aurora's shining dawn,
Bellona was inflaming all mankind   600
And arming savage hands for mortal wounds.
To curb this madness, God has everywhere
Taught nations to accept the selfsame laws
And Romans to become—all by the Rhine
And Danube washed,[67] by Tagus' golden flood,   605

---
64 Cf. Claudian, *De cons. Stil.* 2.354.
65 Cf. Horace, *Satires* 2.3.2.
66 Cf. Lucan, 3.288; Claudian, *De cons. Stil.* 1.152.
67 Cf. Claudian, *De cons. Stil.* 3.13.

The great Ebro and Hesperia's horned stream,[68]
The Ganges and warm Nile with seven mouths.[69]
He bound them by a common law and name
And brought them into bonds of brotherhood.[70]
In all the world they live as citizens   610
Within their native city's sheltering walls,
United round the same ancestral hearth.
Tribes far apart and sundered by the sea
Are brought together through appeals and trials
In common courts, through their commerce and trades   615
In crowded marts, through intermarriage
With those of other climes; for many bloods
Are intermingled in a single race.
These are the fruits of all the victories
Of Roman power: the way, believe me, then   620
Was ready for Christ's coming, which was built
By peace and concord under Roman rule.
Indeed, what place could there have been for God
In such a savage world and in men's hearts
Filled with discord and different views of right?   625
True wisdom visits not the soul of man,
Nor does God enter it when turmoil reigns
Within his senses and disordered mind.
But if the spirit gains supremacy
And curbs the appetites and rebel flesh,   630
Subjects the passions all to reason's sway,
Life then becomes serene, and quiet thoughts
Attract God to the heart that serves one Lord.

Come then, Almighty, to this peaceful earth!
The world united now by peace and Rome   635
Possesses Thee, O Christ. These two you will
To rule all things, but not Rome without peace.

---

68 Cf. Vergil, *Aeneid* 8.77.
69 Cf. *ibid.* 6.800.
70 Cf. Claudian, *De cons. Stil.* 3.150.

Rome's greatness is the cause of that concord,
Which pleases Thee, for sovereign power and fear
Restrain discord and strife. She is not shorn 640
Of former strength nor weakened by old age;
She arms no trembling hands at call of war,
Nor does she with such feeble voice implore
The emperors, as that senator declares,[71]
Who is adept in speech and shrewd conceits 645
And makes a false impression with fine words,
Just as an actor with his wooden mask
Breathes some great evil through its gaping mouth.

If I may take the part of Rome, the words
I speak now in her name befit her more. 650
Since she disdains to mourn her banished gods,
To say the aegis fought for her in war
And that she faints beneath the weight of years,
She hails her princes in a joyful voice:
'I greet you, famous leaders, noble sons 655
Of an unconquered emperor under whom
I shed old age and saw my silver hair
Turn gold again: time blights all mortal things,
But length of days has given me new life,
And I have learned to have no fear of death. 660
At last my years are shown due reverence;
I merit the name of mistress of the world,
When now an olive spray my helmet crowns,
And verdant garlands veil my grim sword-belt,
While, armed, I worship God without bloodshed. 665
Dark Jupiter led me on to crime, alas,
And I profaned my sword, inured to war,
With holy blood of martyrs slain by me.
Nero, inspired by him, his mother killed,
Then drank the Apostles' blood, soiled my fair name 670
With blood of saints and marked me with his crimes.

---

71 Cf. Symmachus, *Relatio* 9.

Then Decius, reveling in his holocausts,
Sated his cruel rage; soon others burned
With thirst to take the lives of noble men
Through grievous wounds and tragic punishments,   675
To pour into my heart a stream of deaths[72]
And cut off innocent heads by court decrees.
Your reign alone has cleansed me of this guilt.
My life is holy now, once impious
Through Jove, I must confess. What cruelty   680
Did he not teach, what good did he demand?
Alarmed at seeing praise of Christ take root,
He burned with wrath and stained the world with blood.[73]
Some dare to blame us for disastrous wars,
Since we have spurned the altars of the gods,   685
And say that Hannibal was driven back[74]
By Mars and Jupiter from the Colline Gate,
That from the Capitol Senones fled
Because the gods fought on the rock above!
Let those who harp upon our past defeats   690
And ancient woes note that in your regime
I suffer no such ills. No savage foe
Knocks at my gates, no strange barbarian
Roams through my captured streets and carries off
My youth in bondage far beyond the Alps.   695

'Of late a Getic king from Danube land
Tried to lay waste to Italy and swore[75]
To raze our citadels, burn our fair shrines,
And clothe our togaed lords in skins of beasts.
Already he had marched across Venetian fields   700
And ravaged rich Liguria, and now
Beyond the Po was pressing on Tuscan soil:

---

72 Cf. Vergil, *Aeneid* 10.908.
73 Cf. *ibid.* 2.502.
74 Cf. Ambrose, *Epist.* 18.4 (Vol. 26, this series); Vergil, *Aeneid* 8.655-656.
75 Cf. Claudian, *De bello Gothico* 81.

No watchful goose drove back the clouds of horse,[76]
Betrayer of the peril in darkness hid,
But men's rude strength, hearts pierced in battle,[77]   705
And courage to face death for fatherland
And to achieve renown mid glorious wounds.[78]
Did that day bring reward for gallantry
Through power of Jove? To lead our troops we had
A youth, mighty in Christ, and Stilicho   710
His guide and father, and Christ was God of both.
Prayer at Christ's altar and the sign of the cross
Foreran the trumpet call: the crest of Christ,
Borne high above the dragons, went before.
The tribe for thirty years Pannonia's scourge[79]   715
Was then wiped out and paid due penalty.
The bodies once adorned with shameful spoils
Now lie in heaps; in centuries to come
Posterity will marvel at the dead
Whose bones have overspread Pollentia's fields.[80]   720
If from the ashes I could lift my head,
By Gauls laid low, if, smoking still, with joy
I hailed my standards at Camillus' return,
If I could deck my dismal halls with wreaths
And with festoons of bay gird crumbling towers,   725
What welcome shall I give you, noble prince,
What flowers strew, what garlands hang in halls,[81]
What banners from my festive portals wave,
I who was free from war, and through your arms[82]
The Gothic onslaught only reached my ears?   730
Mount your triumphal chariot, take your spoils,
And hither come with Christ! Let me remove

---
76 Cf. Ambrose, *Epist.* 18.5 (Vol. 26, this series).
77 Cf. Vergil, *Aeneid* 11.614.
78 Cf. *ibid.* 11.647.
79 Cf. Claudian, *De bello Gothico* 634.
80 Cf. Horace, *Satires* 1.8.16.
81 Cf. Vergil, *Aeneid* 6.884.
82 Cf. *ibid.* 12.559.

The chains from captive throngs, let fall your fetters,[83]
Worn smooth in bondage, matrons and young men!
Let the old man, exiled from home forget   735
His slavery, let the child know he is free,
Now that his mother has returned, let fear
Be banished:[84] we rejoice in victory.
Was such good fortune ours when Carthage's chief
Was routed? After he dashed at our gate,   740
Weakened at Baiae's springs, he lost his strength
In revelry and broke his sword through lust.
But Stilicho in hand to hand conflict
Compelled the ironclad troops to flee from battle.
Here, Christ our God and valor favored us,   745
There, thy delights, Campania, overcame
The wanton foe; bold Fabius was not helped
By Jupiter, but he subdued a tyrant
Already vanquished by Tarentum's charms.
I do not have a worthy recompense[85]   750
For these great services: to honor you
With statues would be idle, for what time
Destroys is worthless; bronze corrodes, bright gold
Decays, the sheen of silver vanishes
And rust and grime discolor precious ores.   755
You merit a living monument, O prince,
For you have sought a glory without end.
Lord of the world, you always will be joined
To Christ and lead my realm to heavenly heights.
Do not be moved by that great orator   760
Who as my legate mourns for rites now dead,
And dares attack our faith with all his powers[86]
Of mind and speech, alas, nor does he see
That you and I are vowed to God, Augustus,
And pagan shrines and altars are ignored.   765

---
83 Cf. Claudian, *De bello Gothico* 616.
84 Cf. Vergil, *Aeneid* 11.14.
85 Cf. Claudian, *De bello Gildonico* 52.
86 Cf. Claudian, *De bello Gothico* 87.

POEMS   165

Let Christ alone defend and rule our halls,
Let no fell demon know the towers of Rome,[87]
But may my court adore the God of peace.'

So speaking, Rome has moved her pious chiefs
To spurn that delegate's distasteful plea,   770
For from the shrine of Jupiter he was sent,
Not by his country, which gives glory to Christ.
Yet he persists in saying that the routes
For seeking one true God are manifold;[88]
That some men seek Him here, some seek Him there,   775
Each by a separate path, but all the ways
Join in the end and come together as one;[89]
That sky and earth, wind, sea, and clouds are given
To all alike, to those who worship Thee,
O Christ, and those who sacrifice to stones.   780
The air, stars, ocean, earth, and rain are held
By all in common, I do not deny.[90]
Beneath one sky the just and the unjust[91]
All dwell, the good and evil breathe one air,
The chaste and the unchaste, the wedded bride   785
And harlot, and the breath that governs life
For priest and gladiator is the same.
The rain cloud driven by the wind in spring
Revives the fields of thief and saint alike.
The traveler and the robber seek pure springs   790
When tired in summer heat, the sea sustains
The pirate and the merchant, waves obey
A foe and bear the thwarts of peaceful ships.
Nature, with power of good or ill, provides
For man's creation and has no regard   795
For merit, since her sole task is nourishment.

---
87 Cf. Claudian, *De cons. Stil.* 3.124.
88 Cf. Symmachus, *Relatio* 10.
89 Cf. Claudian, *In Rufinium* 1.295.
90 Cf. Matt. 5.45.
91 Cf. Tertullian, *op. cit.* 41.3 (Vol. 10, this series).

The world sustains, it does not judge; the Lord
Of nature keeps this function for Himself.
Men now enjoy on like terms the gifts
Once granted them: springs flow and rivers flood,   800
The sail-winged sea is cut by ships, the rain[92]
Showers down, the breezes fly, the air is brisk,
And nature's goods are common to all men,
Long as the elements keep their lawful course,
And so the good man and the criminal   805
Enjoy alike the stars and genial sky.
To live is common, but desert is not.
The Roman, Dahan, Sarmatian, Vandal, Hun,
Gaetulian, German, Saxon, Galaudian,
All walk one earth, the one same sky possess,   810
And ocean that surrounds our whole wide world.[93]
Nay more: the animals drink at our springs;
The dew gives corn to me that gives the grass
To asses, the filthy sow bathes in our stream.
Dogs breathe the air that animates wild beasts.   815
But Roman differs from barbarian
As quadruped from biped, dumb from speaking,
And those who follow God's precepts are far
From foolish cults and superstitious rites,
So sharing air and sky does not create   820
The same religion; it alone sustains
Their bodies and provides for new offspring.
Their kind, their form, their merit matters not,
Provided that these frames are born from earth
And draw their strength from earthly elements,   825
Because the Father's gifts are shed on all
Without distinction and with boundless flow,[94]
And were conferred before the first man sinned.
They are not lessened by the users' faults,

---

92 Cf. Vergil, *Aeneid* 1.574.
93 Cf. Lucan 1.110.
94 Cf. Vergil, *Aeneid* 1.574.

Nor do they shun the shameful and the foul. 830
Likewise, the sun's ray, when it sheds
Its light in every place, strikes golden roofs,
But also shines on thatch begrimed with smoke.
It enters the shining marble Capitol,
But also enters cracks in prison holds, 835
In dung-heap screens and filthy dens of vice.
Yet gloomy prisons will not be the same
As royal ceilings fretted with bright gold.[95]
Those who seek gods in urns and tombs, and shades
Appease with blood, are not the same as those 840
Who worship the Lord of heaven in righteousness
And beautify the temple of their heart.
The secret of mysterious truth, he says,[96]
Cannot be sought except by many paths
And scattered ways, and in the search for God 845
Man must traverse a hundred different roads.
Far other is the truth; for wandering round
Leads to confusion and uncertainty;
One way alone is from all error free,
That with no curves and treacherous bypaths. 850

Yet I confess that at all times two paths
Confront us and that mankind walks two ways,
Not knowing where his faltering step may lead.
One way is many-branched, the other straight:
One leads to God, one follows many gods 855
And has as many forks as images
In shrines, or monstrous phantoms flying round.
It leads some to wand-bearing Bacchus' rites,
Draws others to the Saturnalian feast,
Or shows the worship claimed by infant Jove[97] 860
In hiding mid the cymbals' ringing sound.

---
95 Cf. Statius, *Thebaid* 1.144.
96 Cf. Ambrose, *Epist.* 18.8 (Vol. 26, this series).
97 Cf. Ovid, *Fasti* 4.207-214.

They seek the Lupercalian whips of youth
Who naked run about, and oracles
The frenzied Megalesian eunuch speaks.[98]
Some men, prepared to travel shorter roads, 865
Adore mean plants from gardens by the Nile,
Set leeks and onions in the clouds as gods[99]
And garlic and mustard[100] place above the stars.
For Isis, Serapis, Ape, and Crocodile
Are one with Juno, Laverna, and Priapus: 870
Those Nile adores, these Tiber venerates,
One error, though each wears a different hue.[101]
Shrouded by brush, another pathway looms
Which cattle and dumb woodland creatures tread,
Where blinded man knows nought of heavenly things 875
And lives a captive to a savage fiend.
He thinks there is no God, that all by chance
Is ruled, and ages roll without a guide.[102]
This path is not far distant from the ways
You travel who believe in many gods, 880
A monstrous throng of major deities.
God is the guide along a single way;
He bids mankind to follow one high road
That leads up lofty slopes upon the right.
The path at first is rough, forbidding, dark, 885
And arduous, but pleasant at the end,
Replete with riches and eternal light,
Which amply pay for labors of the past.
Of many tangled paths upon the left
The fiend is guide: this way the bearded sage 890
He drags, that way the man of wealth and fame;

---

98 Cf. Vergil, *Aeneid* 4.376.
99 Cf. Juvenal 15.9.11.
100 Bergman, following the MSS, has *serapen*, 'Serapis,' here. Meyer ('Prudentiana,' *Philologus* 87.349) holds that *senapin* 'Mustard' is a better reading.
101 Cf. Vergil, *Aeneid* 12.8.17.
102 Cf. Juvenal 13.86-88.

With tongues of birds and spells he lures them on,[103]
Incites them with a Sibyl's mutterings,
Drives them to sorcery and magic arts
And frightens them with lying auguries. 895
Do you not see one way with many forks,
Ruled by a guide who will not let you go
To salvation's Lord, but shows the road to death
Along byways with fleeting joys strewn
That end in deep Charybdis' mournful pool?[104] 900
Pagans, depart! You have no right to share
The way with people of God; go far away,
Immerse yourselves in darkness, where that guide
Calls you along the path of infernal night.
We have one way who seek the Lord of life, 905
The way of light, clear day and simple grace.
We walk by hope and faith, seek joys to come,
To which those of this life cannot compare,
For bliss attained does not match that to be.

This is the senator's last sad complaint, 910
That meal to Pallas' altars is denied,
Pay to the Vestals, aid to youthful choirs,
That Vesta's fires are cheated of upkeep.
For this, he says, dry fields bear scanty crops,[105]
Dread famine rages, and throughout the world 915
Mankind grows pale from want and lack of food.
What cruel famine has appeared today,[106]
Sent by Triptolemus and Ceres, wroth
And vengeful at the Vestal's loss of aid,
I cannot think, nor is there any word. 920
I hear the Nile spreads over Egyptian fields
And floods as usual green Canopus' corn.[107]

---
103 Cf. Vergil, *Aeneid* 3.361.
104 Cf. Matt. 7.13,14; Sir. (Ecclus.) 21.10,11.
105 Cf. Symmachus, *Relatio* 11-13.
106 Cf. *ibid.* 15-17; Ambrose, *Epist.* 18.20-21 (Vol. 26, this series).
107 Cf. Vergil, *Georgics* 4.287-288.

News that the river is dry would have been brought,
That parched and dusty barren Memphis lies,
And the Pelusian marsh exhales no fogs. 925
Or has the river's hidden source dried up
So that the spring pours forth a meagre stream?
Has it turned back, refusing to wash our shores,
And bent its course to torrid Indian lands?[108]
Does the dry bed drink up the stream midway, 930
Or sudden crevice swallow up the flood
And keep the tide from covering furrowed lands
And spreading over Egypt's arid plains,
Softening the clods with penetrating surge,
So that the corn may wave on ample fields 935
And clothe them thickly with the heavy ears?[109]
See whether African farmers cease to load
Their ships with grain and send their stacks of wheat
To Tiber's mouth to feed the multitude,
Or Leontinian tillers of the soil 940
Stop launching grain cargoes from Lilybaeum,
Or fleets that bring Sardinian stores to burst
The granaries of Rome no longer sail.[110]
Do Carthaginian yeomen heap their boards
With woodland pears, Sicilians feed on roots, 945
Sardinians furnish acorns from their oaks
And stony cornels form the food of Rome?[111]
Who now comes hungry to the circus shows?
What district suffers want from empty steps,
What mill is silent on Janiculum?[112] 950
What great provisions every province brings,
What harvests from the earth's rich bosom flow
Is shown by bread you give your people, Rome,
Which feeds the sloth of such great multitudes.

---

108 Cf. *ibid.* 293.
109 Cf. Claudian, *De raptu Pros.* 1.190.
110 Cf. Vergil, *Georgics* 1.49.
111 Cf. Vergil, *Aeneid* 3.649-650; *Georgics* 1.300; 2.34; Tibullus 2.1.38
112 Public grain-mills were located on the Janiculum.

That one year is less fruitful than the last 955
Is nothing strange or novel in this world:
Our fathers often learned to suffer want
When wind and burning sun dried up the clouds
And frequent rain did not pour showers in spring
On young green crops; when corn matured 960
Before the tender grains had swelled with milk,
For sap was checked by hot winds from the east,
So that the stalks were bare, and sterile straw
Deceived and brought the farmer's hopes to nought.
The land was prone to failures such as these 965
Ere the Palladium and Vesta saved
The household gods of Troy with hidden fire,[113]
Before the sire of Priam built his walls,
Before the maiden Pallas Athens raised,
For in these cities, as they say, was lit 970
The Vestal fire, caught from the primal spark,
And sacred hearths by Trojans and Greeks were fed.[114]
The elements fail because of ancient sin,
And driven from their normal course, they bring
Mishaps contrary to the yearly law. 975
Now rust, caused by bad air, devours the crop,
Now after west winds in a sunny spring
A cold blast from the north bombards the corn
And taints the blighted grain with sooty smut,
Or as the blade sprouts from the tender seed, 980
It is destroyed by frequent killing frosts
And cannot thrust its root into the soil;
Pushed from the earth by penetrating cold,
The bare stem lies uncovered on the ground.
Then thorny caltraps and the thistles grow, 985
One caused by drought, and one by too much rain.
The weather more or less extreme gives rise
To all these ills of earth and wounds the world.

---
113 Cf. Vergil, *Aeneid* 5.743-744.
114 Cf. *ibid.* 2.293-297.

Likewise, the body's evil conduct leads
To sickness, and neglect of nature's laws   990
Afflicts the members through want of control.
The order of the world and of our frame
Is one; the selfsame nature upholds both.
From nothing made, they grow, doomed to return
To nothing and succumb to disease or age;   995
Not free from fault is nature that will end.
Trust me, the sky has always woven years
Of varied fruitfulness: some with rich crops
It has endowed, some doomed to barrenness
That rendered vain the farmer's hope and toil.   1000
But if this drought caused by a fickle earth
Avenges now the wrongs of Vestal maids,
Why are not fields of Christians only spoiled,
Through whom your virgins' stipends are refused?
We profit from the tillage of our land   1005
And fret not at our toil: and if a stone
Stood there that pagans once with ribbons bound
Or worshiped with the lung of victim hen,
It has been shattered; Terminus is profaned,
And vengeful ax has felled the tree once decked   1010
With fillets that upheld the smoking lamps.
And yet the yield from farmlands is not less,
Nor sunny weather less serene and bright,
Nor wind decreased that showers fields with rain.
Our frugal lives do not have many needs,   1015
And when crops thrive we are not overjoyed,
Nor do we take delight in sordid gain.
To those who place their hope in endless joy
The good things of this present life are slight.
Thrice happy is the prudent husbandman[115]   1020
Who tills his land and soul and spends on both
Unsleeping care, like laborers in the field
Whom Christ, the Master, taught by these precepts:

---
[115] Cf. *ibid.* 4.657; *Georgics* 2.458; Horace, *Satires* 2.2.3.

'When you in furrows sow your seed, avoid[116]
The rocky ground and let no seed fall there,
Because at first the shoot will make quick growth,
But when the sap withdraws, the thirsty plant
Will be all withered by the fiery sun.[117]
Let seeds not fall among the thorny shrubs[118]
For their sharp sprays mix with the growing corn,
And piercing brambles choke the tender stalks.[119]
Then on the highway scatter not the grains[120]
For these lie bare to be devoured by birds[121]
And are abandoned to the sport of crows.'
God guides the farmer by these wise precepts;
The plowman heeds the Heavenly Father's law,
But plans his crops both of his soul and land
So that his heart will not shine less within
Than bounteous harvests in his smiling fields.
For we root out the briers from the heart
Lest vicious brambles kill the living sprout,
Lest prickly thorns of crime and evil choke
The harvest of the soul with frequent sin,
Lest rocky barren sand dry up the faith[122]
That withers in the heart, or passion burn
Within the breast and scorch the gifts of grace,
Lest base desire leave little place for God,
Lest hope on which our inner spirit is fed
Be given as food to unclean birds, and faith
Be cast away as prey of our winged foe.
Such care will cause our fields to bring forth fruit
A hundredfold,[123] when ardently pursued
Without fear that the worms may gnaw the store

---

116 Cf. Vergil, *Georgics* 1.223.
117 Cf. Matt. 13.5,6.
118 Cf. Matt. 13.7.
119 Cf. Vergil, *Georgics* 1.76.
120 Cf. Vergil, *Aeneid* 5.273.
121 Cf. Matt. 13.4.
122 Cf. Vergil, *Georgics* 2.212.
123 Cf. Matt. 13.8.

Or black ants lay it up deep in their holes.[124]
Our virgins are endowed with splendid gifts:[125]   1055
Reserve, face hidden with a holy veil,
Integrity and charm not seen abroad,
Frugal repasts and spirit always calm,
And vow of chastity that ends with life.
Hence fruit a hundredfold comes to their barns,[126]   1060
Barns not exposed to thieves that prowl at night,
For no thief enters heaven, and celestial doors
Are not unlocked by fraud, which dwells on earth.

How worthy is the Vestals' chastity,
I now shall prove, and how it is observed.   1065
First, they are chosen in their tender years
Before the love of chastity and the gods
Inclines them of their own free will and choice
To spurn the lawful bonds of marriage.
Their purity is on thankless altars placed,   1070
And joys of flesh are absent, not from scorn,
But from loss; the body, not the mind, is pure,
Nor does the bed bring rest on which the maid[127]
Laments her wound and loss of nuptial ties.
Since hope remains, love's fire does not grow cold,   1075
For one day wedding torches may be lit,
And graying heads may wear the bridal veil.
For an appointed time Vesta enjoins
Virginity, but scorns a chaste old age.
While youthful vigor favored marriage bonds,   1080
Love was not made fruitful in motherhood.
Her sacred task fulfilled, the Vestal weds;
She leaves behind the hearth her youth has served,
And brings her wrinkles to the nuptial couch,
Where only tepid joys are known to her.   1085

---
124 Cf. Matt. 6.19; Vergil, *Georgics* 1.185.
125 Cf. Ambrose, *Epist.* 18.12 (Vol. 26, this series).
126 Cf. Matt. 13.8.
127 Cf. Vergil, *Aeneid* 6.600.

But while the fillet binds her flowing locks,
And the virgin priestess tends prophetic fires,
She is borne through the streets with solemn pomp,
Reclining in a cushioned car,[128] and shows
Her unveiled face to wondering eyes of Rome. 1090
Thence in her chaste and bloodless piety
She to the amphitheatre goes to view
The bloody fights and human deaths, and looks
With holy eyes on wounds received for bread.[129]
She sits there, fillet crowned, enjoying the shows. 1095
O soft and tender heart! At blows she stands,
And when a victor stabs his rival's throat,
She calls him her delight;[130] the gentle maid
Bids him by thumb turned up to strike his foe,[131]
So that no breath of life may in him stay, 1100
While from the thrust he gasps in agony.
Does their fame lie in this, that they always
Keep watch for Rome's imperial majesty,
That they protect the people and the lords,
That they dispose their tresses on their necks, 1105
And bind their brows with snoods and braid their hair,[132]
Because, with ghosts as witness under ground,
They slay the ox above the flames and pray?[133]
Is it that, from their seats in the balcony,
They see the blows of the three-pronged javelin strike 1110
The gladiator's face, and from his wounds
How he bedews the arena on his side
And prints his tracks with blood as he withdraws?[134]

---

128 Cf. Ambrose, *Epist.* 18.11-12 (Vol. 26, this series); Vergil, *Aeneid* 8.665-666.
129 Free men often volunteered as gladiators and received pay for their services.
130 The heroes of the arena were especially the ladies favorites; cf. Tertullian, *Spectacles* 95n. (Vol. 40, this series).
131 Cf. Juvenal 3.36-37.
132 Cf. Vergil, *Georgics* 1.185.
133 Cf. Vergil, *Aeneid* 11.199; 12.214; Tertullian, *De spectaculis*, 5.7 (Vol. 40, this series).
134 Cf. Vergil, *Georgics* 3.171.

I pray you, lord of the Ausonian realm,
That golden Rome may know such crimes no more,   1115
And that this rite be banned like all the rest.
Does not your father's glory lack this crown,
Which God and paternal love have kept for you?
That he alone might not receive the praise
For this great boon, he said: 'My son, I keep   1120
A part for you,' and left the honor all to you.
Accept, O prince, this glory of your reign,
And as your father's heir, receive this praise.
He banned the deluge of Rome with blood of bulls:
Do you forbid grim human sacrifice.   1125
Let no man die in Rome as sport for crowds,
Nor Vestals feast their eyes on cruel deaths.
Now let the circus be content with beasts
And slaughter of men no longer entertain.[135]
Let Rome praise God and honor her great prince,   1130
Let her be just and free from every crime,
Let her be like her chief in piety.

---

[135] The emperor, Honorius, abolished the gladiatorial combats in 404.

SCENES FROM SACRED HISTORY, OR TWOFOLD NOURISHMENT

(TITULI HISTORIARUM, QUI 'DITTOCHAEI' NOMINE CIRCUMFERUNTUR)

SCENES FROM SACRED HISTORY, OR TWOFOLD NOURISHMENT

1. *Adam and Eve*

In the beginning Eve was as white as a dove, but was after
Stained by the serpent's dark venom when he enticed
   her to evil,
And in turn she infected with foul taint the innocent
   Adam;
Then the victorious snake gives them fig leaves to
   cover their nudeness.[1]

2. *Cain and Abel*

God receives in a different manner the gifts of two
   brothers,[2]   5
Giving approval to animal life and rejecting the earth's
   fruits.
Out of envy the husbandman slays the shepherd: In Abel
Is the type of the soul; in the offering of Cain, that of body.

3. *Noe and the Flood*

As a sign that the flood had abated the dove is now
   bringing

---
1 Cf. Gen. 3.6-21.
2 Cf. Gen. 4.3-5.

Back to the ark in her beak the budding green branch
  of an olive.³   10
For the raven, held captive by gluttony, clung to foul
  bodies,⁴
While the dove brought back the glad tidings of peace
  that was given.

4. *Abraham and His Guest*

This is the lodging place of the Lord, where an oak
  branch at Mambre⁵
Covered the pastoral roof of the ancient seer; in this
  hospice
Sara laughed at the joy of bearing a child in her old age   15
And at the faith her venerable husband could have in
  the marvel.

5. *The Tomb of Sara*

Abraham purchased a field wherein he might bury his
  wife's bones,⁶
Inasmuch as justice and faith on the earth dwell
  as strangers:
This is the cave for which he expended a great sum
  of money,⁷
To prepare a fit resting place for his wife's holy ashes.⁸   20

---

3 Cf. Gen. 8.8,11.
4 Cf. Gen. 8.7.
5 Cf. Gen. 18.1,10.
6 Cf. Gen. 23.4,16.
7 Cf. Horace, *Epist.* 2.2.165.
8 Cf. Vergil, *Aeneid* 3.495; 7.598.

6. The Dream of Pharao

Seven ears of corn twice appearing to Pharao in slumber[9]
And a like number of cattle foretell by their differing
    symbols[10]
Times of plenty and famine disposed in seven year
    periods.
This is the meaning the patriarch gave through
    Christ's revelation.

7. Joseph Recognized by His Brothers

Sold through a plot of his brothers, that same boy
    in secret[11]   25
Gives command that a cup in a sack of grain should
    be hidden;
Then when Joseph arrests them for theft, their betrayal
    is made known.[12]
Recognizing their brother, they are put to shame by
    his pardon.[13]

8. The Burning Bush

God in the form of a flame that hovered over the briers,[14]
With His face all glorious, called to a youth who
    was guarding   30
Flocks at the time; as bidden, the youth lifts his rod
    now a serpent;[15]

---

9 Cf. Gen. 41.17-31.
10 Cf. Claudian, *De raptu Pros.* 2.45.
11 Cf. Gen. 37.28.
12 Cf. Gen. 44.2-12.
13 Cf. Gen. 45.3,4.
14 Cf. Exod. 3.2.
15 Cf. Exod. 4.3.

He unfastens his shoes and to Pharao's court he then
    hurries.[16]

9. *The Passage of the Sea*

Safely the upright man makes his way even through
    the deep waters.[17]
Lo, for the servants of God the Red Sea is parted asunder,
While the same billows engulf the frenzied plotters of evil.   35
Pharao is overwhelmed, but the path lay open for Moses.

10. *Moses has Received the Law*

With the celestial fire the top of the mountain is
    smoking,[18]
Where the tables of stone with the ten commandments
    are given
Unto Moses; receiving the Law he returns to his people,
But their god is a golden calf, a god made of metal.[19]   40

11. *The Manna and the Quails*

By the bread of angels the tents of our fathers are
    whitened.[20]
Faith in this wonder is sure; for a golden vessel holds
    manna
Kept since that time;[21] another cloud now descends on
    the ingrates,
And the flocks of quails satisfy their hunger for fleshpots.[22]

---

16 Cf. Exod. 3.5; 7.9.
17 Cf. Exod. 14.27-29.
18 Cf. Exod. 19.18.
19 Cf. Exod. 32.7.
20 Cf. Exod. 16.14.
21 Cf. Exod. 16.33,34.
22 Cf. Exod. 16.13.

12. *The Brazen Serpent in the Wilderness*

On the dry way through the wilderness fiery serpents
   were swarming,[23] 45
And their venomous bites made wounds that were killing
   the people,
But a brazen serpent is hung on a cross by their leader
To remove all the strength of the venom and heal the
   afflicted.

13. *The Pool of Myrrh in the Wilderness*

To the thirsting people the taste of the pool was revolting,[24]
For as bitter as gall were the stagnant waters it contained. 50
Saintly Moses instructs them: 'Bring me a piece of that
   firewood;
Throw it into the pool and the gall will be turned into
   sweetness.'

14. *The Grove of Elim in the Wilderness*

Led by Moses the people came to a grove with six
   fountains[25]
And six others again that with their crystalline waters
Flooded the seventy palm trees; that mystic oasis of Elim 55
Was a symbol also of the number of apostles in Scripture.

15. *The Twelve Stones in the Jordan*

Jordan with refluent stream to its source is carried
   back swiftly,

---
23 Cf. Num. 21.6-9.
24 Cf. Exod. 15.23-25.
25 Cf. Exod. 15.27.

Leaving the people of God a dry path to be trod in
   their crossing;[26]
You may see here the twelve stones that our fathers set
   in the river
To prefigure the twelve disciples one day to be chosen.[27]   60

16. *The House of Rahab the Harlot*

Jericho has fallen and Rahab's house only is standing.[28]
Hostess of holy men, the harlot—so great is faith's
   virtue—
Safe in her unscathed home, exposes the cord of bright
   scarlet
In the face of the flames as a sign of the blood of salvation.

17. *Samson*

Samson resistless because of his hair is attacked by a lion;[29]   65
When he killed the wild beast, from its mouth there
   flowed streams of honey,
And from an ass's jawbone comes forth a fountain of water:
Folly with water overflows and virtue with sweetness.

18. *Samson*

Samson catches three hundred foxes and arms them
   with firebrands,[30]
Which he ties to their tails, and he lets them go into the
   cornfields   70

---
26 Cf. Jos. 3.14-17.
27 Cf. Jos. 4.8.
28 Cf. Jos. 2.1,18-21; 6.17,25.
29 Cf. Judges, 14.5-8; 15.19.
30 Cf. Judges 15.4,5.

Of the Philistines to burn their crops: thus the fox of
    false doctrine
Cunningly scatters the flames of heresy over our vineyards.

19. *David*

David was young, the last of his brothers and now as
    he guarded
Jesse's flocks, he was tuning the harp that was soon to
    give pleasure
To the king.[31] In the course of time he wages fierce battles   75
And with a whizzing sling he defeats the giant Goliath.[32]

20. *The Reign of David*

David's royal insignia shine with marvelous brightness:
Scepter and oil and crown, robe of purple and altar,
They are all proper to Christ, the mantle and crown and
    the scepter,
Symbol of power, the horn of the cross, the altar and oil.   80

21. *The Building of the Temple*

Wisdom builds up a temple through Solomon's faithful
    obedience,
And the queen of the South brings hither a heap of
    gold talents.[33]
For the time is at hand when Christ shall build his own
    temple
In the heart of man to be reverenced by Greeks and
    barbarians.

---
31 Cf. 1 Kings 16.17-23.
32 Cf. 1 Kings 17.49,50.
33 Cf. 3 Kings 10.1-10.

22. *The Sons of the Prophets*

While the sons of the prophets chanced to be cutting
    down timber[34]   85
On the banks of the river, an axe-head fell from its
    handle.
Down to the bottom the iron sank, but a piece of
    light firewood,
Thrown into the water, soon brought it again to the
    surface.

23. *The Hebrews Led into Captivity*

Captive because of their many transgressions the race
    of the Hebrews
Mourned their sad exile by the cruel rivers of Babylon;[35]   90
They disregarded the order to sing the songs of their
    nation,
Hanging their tuneful harps on the bitter willow tree's
    branches.[36]

24. *The House of King Ezechias*

Pious Ezechias merited here the delay for fifteen years[37]
Of the day of his death that the will of God had
    appointed;[38]
This was confirmed by the sun as it turned to the
    eastern horizon,   95
Shedding its light on the spaces the evening shadows
    had covered.

---

[34] Cf. 4 Kings 6.5-7.
[35] Cf. Ps. 136.1.
[36] Cf. Ps. 136.2; Vergil, *Eclogues* 1.78.
[37] Cf. 4 Kings 20.1-11.
[38] Cf. Seneca, *Hercules furens* 190.

25. *The Angel Gabriel is Sent to Mary*

When God's coming draws near,[39] the angel Gabriel
    advances
From the Father's high throne and enters the house
    of the virgin.
'Mary,' he says, 'the Holy Spirit will render thee fruitful,
And thou shalt give birth to the Christ, O glorious
    Virgin.'[40]   100

26. *The City of Bethlehem*

Head of the world is holy Bethlehem that brought forth
    Jesus,[41]
Source of creation and fountain Himself of every
    beginning.
This is the city that gave birth to Christ as man, yet
    the Christ lived
Ever as God ere the sun or the morning star was created.

27. *The Gifts of the Magi*

Here the Magi bring to the Christ child, nursed by
    the Virgin,[42]   105
Precious offerings of myrrh and of gold and of
    sweet-smelling incense.
That such great reverence is shown to her chaste womb,
    the mother now marvels.
And that she has borne the God-Man, who is King
    of Creation.

---

39 Cf. Vergil, *Aeneid* 6.258.
40 Cf. Luke 1.26-33.
41 Cf. Matt. 2.6.
42 Cf. Matt. 2.11; Juvencus 1.282-86 (PL 19.98).

28. The Shepherds Warned by the Angels

Light angelic bedazzles the watchful eyes of the
 shepherds,[43]
Making known the good tidings that Christ has been born
 of a virgin. 110
They find Him wrapped in swaddling clothes, and His
 crib was a manger;
They exult with great joy and kneeling, they worship
 his Godhead.

29. The Massacre of the Infants at Bethlehem

Herod, the impious enemy, slaughters innumerable
 infants,[44]
As he furiously rages in search of the Christ-child
 among them.
Cradles reek with the milky blood of the innocent
 children 115
And the hot gashes moisten the loving breasts of the
 mothers.

30. The Baptism of Christ

John the Baptist, sustained by locusts and honey
 from woodlands
And attired in a mantle of camel's hair was baptizing
In the stream; he had baptized Christ when the Spirit
 from heaven
Witnessed that He who was baptized forgives the sins
 of the baptized.[45] 120

---

43 Cf. Luke 2.8-20.
44 Cf. Matt. 2.16.
45 Cf. Matt. 3.13-17.

31. *The Pinnacle of the Temple*

Still the pinnacle stands, outlasting the temple's destruction,
For the corner raised up from that stone which the builders rejected[46]
Will remain throughout all ages forever and ever;
Now it is head of the temple and holds the new stones together.

32. *Water Changed into Wine*

Once the Galileans were celebrating a marriage,[47]   125
Crowded with witnesses, when the servants saw the wine failing;
Christ bids them quickly fill the water-pots with clear water,
And an abundance of mellow wine is now poured from the tankards.

33. *The Pool of Siloe*

Cure for disease is that water which by the Spirit is stirred up
In a dark manner at various hours; Siloe men called it.[48]   130
Here the Savior anointed the eyes of the blind man with spittle,
And He bade him to go and wash in that fountain of water.

---

46 Cf. Matt. 4.5-7; 21.42. Commenting on the ambiguity of this quatrain, Lavarenne suggests that it may refer to the temptation of Christ when Satan took Him up to the pinnacle of the temple, or to the discourse of Christ in the temple recounted in Chapter 21 of St. Matthew's Gospel.
47 Cf. John 2.1-10.
48 Cf. John 5.3,4; 9.6-11. Prudentius here confuses the pool of Siloe with that at Bethsaida, as in the *Apothesis* 1.680. (Cf. *supra*, p. 28).

34. *The Passion of John the Baptist*

Sinister tribute the dancing girl demands as her guerdon,[49]
Head of the Baptist cut off to carry back on a platter
To the lap of her shameless mother; the royal performer   135
Bears the gift, with her hands all bespattered with blood
    of the just one.

35. *Christ Walks on the Sea*

In the midst of the sea the Lord walks, and while
    treading the waters[50]
He commands his disciple to leave the tottering vessel,
But the man's mortal misgiving causes his footsteps to
    falter;[51]
Christ by the hand now leads him and steadies the feet
    that are sinking.[52]   140

36. *The Demon is Sent into the Swine*

In his sepulchral prison the savage demon had broken[53]
Fetters of iron that bound him; he darts forth and kneels
    before Jesus.
But the Lord sets the man free and orders the devil
    to madden
Herds of the swine and to plunge with them into the
    depths of the vast sea.

---

49 Cf. Matt. 14.6-11.
50 Cf. Vergil, *Aeneid* 12.452.
51 Cf. Matt. 14.25-32.
52 Cf. Vergil, *Aeneid* 3.659.
53 Cf. Mark 5.1-13; Luke 8.27-33.

37. *The Five Loaves and Two Fishes*

God has broken five loaves and two fishes and fed the
   five thousand[54]   145
With these viands that satisfy to the fullest their hunger.
Then twice six baskets are filled with the fragments that
   are left over:
Such is the bounty dispensed from the heavenly table
   forever.

38. *Lazarus is Raised from the Dead*

There is at Bethany a spot that witnessed a glorious
   miracle,[55]
When it saw thee, O Lazarus, return from the region
   of darkness.   150
One may behold the burial place with its portals now
   broken,
Whence your members returned from the grave with
   its ghastly corruption.

39. *The Field of Blood*

Sold for the price of a heinous crime, Haceldama's
   garden,[56]
Filled with graves, receives men's earthly remains for
   interment.
This is the price of the blood of Christ. The miserable
   Judas   155
Draws the halter about his neck to atone for his outrage.[57]

---
54 Cf. Matt. 14.15-21.
55 Cf. John 11.1-44.
56 Cf. Matt. 27.7,8; Acts 1.19.
57 Cf. Matt. 27.5; Acts 1.18.

40. *The House of Caiphas*

Lo, the house of the wicked blasphemer, Caiphas, has fallen,
Where the sacred face of the Christ was cruelly smitten.[58]
This destruction will be the lot of all reprobate sinners,
For their life will lie buried in crumbling ruins forever. 160

41. *The Pillar at Which Christ was Scourged*

In this house the Lord stood upright, bound and tied
   to a pillar,
And submitted His back as a slave to the pitiless
   scourging.[59]
Worthy of reverence, this pillar still stands, supporting
   a temple,[60]
And instructing us how to lead our lives free from all
   scourges.

42. *The Passion of the Savior*

Water and blood flow forth from the transpierced sides
   of the Savior:[61]   165
Blood betokens the victory, water stands for baptism.
Then the two robbers on crosses on each side dispute with
   each other:[62]
One denies Christ is God, the other wins heavenly glory.

---

58 Cf. Matt. 26.57-67; Mark 14.53-65.
59 Cf. Mark 15.15.
60 Cf. Jerome, *Epist.* 108.9.
61 Cf. John 19.34.
62 Cf. Luke 23.39-43.

43. The Sepulcher of Christ[63]

Neither the stone nor the bolts of the tomb could hold
  Christ a captive;[64]
Death lies conquered by Him, He has trampled on hell's
  fiery chasm.   170
With Him a throng of saints ascended to heavenly regions,
And to many He showed Himself, letting them see Him
  and touch Him.

44. The Mount of Olives

From the Mountain of Olives Christ returned to the
  Father,[65]
And He left the footmarks of peace impressed on its
  summit.[66]
From the eternal branches there flows a copious liquor,   175
Which attests that the earth has been washed by the gifts
  of the chrism.[67]

45. The Passion of Stephen

Stephen is first to receive the crown for his blood
  shed as a martyr,[68]
Dashed to the earth by a rain of stones. But while he lies
  bleeding

---

[63] The authenticity of this quatrain has been questioned, since it does not appear in the manuscripts and first editions and was first printed by Geselinus and Fabricius in the sixteenth century.
[64] Cf. Matt. 27.52,53; 28.1-10; Luke 24.39,40; John 20.27; Acts 1.3.
[65] Cf. Acts 1.9.
[66] According to tradition a stone kept in an oratory built by St. Helena on the Mount of Olives bears the imprint of the foot of Christ.
[67] Baptism.
[68] Cf. Acts 7.57-59.

Under the cobbles, he prays to Christ not to charge his
    assailants
With the stoning. How wondrous the love of that great
    protomartyr!   180

46. *The Beautiful Gate*

Standing still is the gate of the temple which men
    called Beautiful;[69]
Glorious work of Solomon it was, but at that portal
Shone a more splendid work of Christ, for the voice of
    Peter
Bade a lame man arise, who ran about leaping with
    wonder.

47. *The Vision of Peter*

Peter sees in a dream a vessel descending from heaven,[70]   185
Filled with all kinds of animals: he refuses to eat them,
But the Lord commands him to look on all things as
    wholesome.
He arises and calls unclean tribes to the heavenly mysteries.

48. *The Vessel of Election*

He who was once a ravening wolf is now clothed as a
    soft lamb:[71]
He who was Saul is changed into Paul when he loses his
    vision.   190
Then he receives his sight once more and becomes an
    apostle,

---

69 Cf. Acts 3.2-10.
70 Cf. Acts 10.9-15; 34-46.
71 Cf. Acts 9.3-5; Gen. 49.27.

Teacher of Gentiles, with power of speech to change
   crows into white doves.

49. *The Apocalypse of John*

Twenty-four elders here seated, resplendent with vessels
   of incense,
Harps, and crowns of glory, the Lamb of God are
   acclaiming,[72]
Who was stained by the blood of His Passion and is
   alone able
To examine the book and its seven seals break asunder.[73]

---

[72] Cf. Apoc. 4.4; 5.8.
[73] Cf. Apoc. 5.1-6.

EPILOGUE

EPILOGUE

God, the Father, unto Thee
The saintly man, pure, innocent, and faithful,
  Offers gifts of holy thoughts
That in his blissful heart and spirit flourish.
  One deprives himself of wealth   5
That he may from his store sustain the needy.
  Swift iambics I devote,
To which I join the quick-revolving trochees,
  For I own no sanctity
Nor gold to ease the pauper's want and misery.   10
  God, however, deigns to smile
On my dull song and to it kindly harkens.
  Halls of rich men are adorned
With vessels set in every nook and corner:[1]
  Here the golden goblet shines,   15
And there the splendid bowl of burnished copper;
  Here the jar of earthenware,
And there the massive tray of lustrous silver,
  Many a vase of ivory
And wooden platters carved from oak and elm.   20
  Every vessel is of worth
That lends itself to service of the master,[2]
  For his house contains as well
The costly urn and simple wooden trencher.
  In His Father's heavenly court   25
Christ welcomes me, a crumbling, worn out vessel
  Meet for lowly offices,

---

[1] Cf. 2 Tim. 2.20; Tacitus, *Dial.* 22.4.
[2] Cf. 2 Tim. 2.21; Rom. 9.21.

And lets me stand in some secluded corner.
　　Lo, I am but earthenware
Within the royal palace of salvation,　　　　　　　　　30
　　Yet that I have given to God
The smallest service brings me boundless comfort.
　　Come what may, I will rejoice
That feeble lips of mine have sung Christ's praises,
　　[Christ, the ruler of my life.]³　　　　　　　　35

---

3 Bergman brackets this line, which he regards as the addition of a copyist. The Hipponactean couplet used here by Prudentius consists of a shorter trochaic dimeter catalectic line followed by a longer iambic dimeter catalectic line. The poem would, therefore, normally end with the longer line.

GENERAL INDEX

Aaron, *2:* 98, 109
Abel, *1:* 160, 226; *2:* 43, 179
Abraham, *1:* 76, 85; *2:* 6, 17, 18, 79, 80, 180
Abram, *2:* 79
Absalom, *2:* 62, 63
abstinence, *1:* 45, 46, 47
Achan, *2:* 98
Acheron, *1:* 36
Acislus, *1:* 138
Acta Proconsularia, *1:* 267 n., 272 n.
Actium, *2:* 157
Adam, *1:* 20, 60, 67, 217; *2:* 28, 35, 38, 66, 71, 88, 166, 179
Adonis, *1:* 200
Adrian I, *1:* 252 n.
Aemilianus, *1:* 170
Aeneas, *1:* 123 n.; *2:* 20, 125, 158
Aeolia, *2:* 125
Aescalapius, *1:* 202; *2:* 12
Africa, *1:* 138, 270, 273; *2:* 20, 122, 152, 156, 170
Agnes, St., *1:* 274, 276, 277, 279
Alamo, Mateo, *1:* x, 241 n.
Alba, *1:* 256
Alcala, *1:* 139
Alcides, *2:* 123
Alcmena, *1:* 200
Algidus, *2:* 157
Allard, Paul, *1:* x, xi n., xii n., xxi n., xxvi n., 95 n., 240 n., 241 n., 250 n.
Alleluia, *1:* 28
Almo, *1:* 197
Alps, *1:* 126; *2:* 130
altar, *1:* 37, 55, 87, 107, 124, 137, 145, 147, 165, 189, 193, 254, 258, 271; *2:* 43, 57, 79, 105, 107, 163, 185
Amalec, *1:* 91
Amalthaea, *1:* 217
Ambrose, St., *1:* xi n., 3 n., 4 n., 7 n., 8 n., 9 n., 10 n., 11 n., 15 n., 17 n., 22 n., 30 n., 36 n., 40 n., 45 n., 54 n., 67 n., 68 n., 71 n., 75 n., 76 n., 87 n., 107 n., 111 n., 121 n., 184 n., 240 n., 274 n., 275 n., 276 n., 278 n.; *2:* 43 n., 142 n., 152 n., 156 n., 162 n., 163 n., 167 n., 174 n., 175 n.
Amen, *1:* 28, 256 n.
Ammon, *2:* 20, 152
Amorrhite, *2:* 58
Amphitryon, *1:* 200

INDEX

Amyclae, 2: 158
Ana, 1: 136
Ancus, 2: 122
angels, 1: 12, 24, 27, 28, 61, 101, 130, 138, 144, 157, 213, 239, 278; 2: 7, 23, 24, 34, 50, 68, 73, 80, 148, 187
Anicius, 2: 133
Annius, 2: 133
Annunciation, 2: 24, 187
Antichrist, 1: 43
Antinous, 2: 124
Antiochus, 2: 158
Anubis, 2: 12, 157
Apelles, 2: 142
Apodemus, 1: 144
Apollo, 1: 132; 2: 19, 20, 124, 158
Apostles, 1: 29, 91, 123, 260; 2: 8, 107, 114, 161, 183, 184, 190, 194
Appenines, 2: 157
Appian Way, 1: 266 n.
Arcadia, 2: 123
Arcadius, 2: 141 n.
Arevalus, 1: xxvi, 4 n., 12 n., 16 n., 26 n., 39 n., 43 n., 66 n., 86 n., 91 n., 99 n., 145 n.
Argo, 2: 119
Argos, 2: 156
Ariadne, 2: 120
Aristo, 1: 229, 233
Aristotle, 2: 12
Arius, 2: 106
Arles, 1: 139
Armellini, 1: 252 n.
Arnobius, 2: 129 n.
Arpinum, 2: 132
Ascension, 1: 23, 60 n., 68, 193, 217
Asclepiades, 1: 192, 195, 207, 214, 219, 230
Asia, 2: 157
Assyria, 2: 10, 59, 83, 158
Astyanax, 1: 220 n.
Athanasius, St., 2: 14 n., 15 n.
Athens, 2: 152, 171
Atlas, 2: 20
Attic, 1: 35
Attis, 2: 142
Augurius, 1: 138 n., 168, 175
August, 1: 258
Augustine, St., 1: xxix n., 6 n., 11 n., 18 n., 22 n., 36 n., 38 n., 55 n., 69 n., 72 n., 106 n., 111 n., 119 n., 121 n., 129 n., 146 n., 168 n., 172 n., 183 n., 260 n., 267 n., 272 n., 274 n., 275 n.; 2: 26 n., 128 n.
Augustus, 1: 110, 199 n.; 2: 123, 125, 164
Aurora, 2: 159
Ausonia, 2: 133, 176
Ausonius, 1: 4 n., 14 n., 15 n., 17 n., 23 n.
Aventine, 2: 120
Avernus, 2: 71, 75, 128

Baal, 1: 92; 2: 16
Babylon, 1: 26, 173; 2: 9, 59, 158, 186
Bacchus, 1: 203 n.; 2: 120, 122, 135, 167
Bactra, 2: 25
Baiae, 2: 164
baptism, 1: 11, 44, 49, 120, 169, 180 n., 181, 209, 263; 2: 21, 28, 34, 84, 134, 188, 192
baptistery, 1: 180, 262 n., 263; 2: 134 n.

INDEX

Barcelona, *1:* 139
Barula, *1:* 190 n.
Basil, St., *1:* xxxi n., 3 n., 14 n., 17 n., 19 n., 28 n., 39 n., 45 n.
basilica, *1:* xiii, 81 n., 126 n., 257 n., 262, 264 n., 274 n., 275 n.; *2:* 134 n.
Bassus, *2:* 133
Bayo, M. J., *1:* xxvi
Beelzebub, *1:* 156
Belial, *2:* 61, 64, 103
Bellona, *2:* 98, 159
Bergman, J., *1:* x, xii n., xiii n., xiv, xv n., xxvi, 19 n., 70 n., 75 n., 86 n., 89 n., 145 n., 241 n.; *2:* 11 n., 47 n., 80 n., 104 n., 151 n., 168 n., 200 n.
Bethany, *2:* 191
Bethsaida, *2:* 28 n., 189 n.
Bethlehem, *1:* 45, 81 n., 87, 88, 222; *2:* 187, 188
Boaz, *2:* 69
Brennus, *2:* 158
Britons, *1:* 273
Bromius, *2:* 120, 156
Brutus, *2:* 133

Caesar, *1:* 98, 100, 106, 109, 110, 149, 150; *2:* 124
Caiphas, *2:* 179, 192
Cain, *1:* 43, 44, 45; *2:* 179
Calahorra, *1:* ix, x, xx, 95, 139, 180, 241 n.
Callistus, St., *1:* 24, 241 n., 242 n.
Camillus, *1:* 106; *2:* 158, 163
Campania, *1:* 256; *2:* 164
Candida Massa, *1:* 272 n.
Cannae, *2:* 158
Canopus, *1:* 202; *2:* 169

Capitol, *2:* 20, 121, 123, 132, 136, 162, 167
Capua, *1:* 256
Carrhae, *2:* 159
Carthage, *1:* 138, 140 n., 266 n., 269, 271; *2:* 156, 164, 170
Cassian, St., of Imola, *1:* xx, 182, 184, 188, 189
Cassian, Monk, *1:* 4 n., 8 n., 30 n.
Cassian, St., of Tangier, *1:* 139
Catholic Church, *1:* 243; *2:* 15, 115
Catholic faith, *1:* xxxi, 176, 242
Catiline, *2:* 132
Cato, *1:* 122; *2:* 133
Catullus, *1:* 199 n.
Caucasus, *2:* 19
Cecropian, *1:* 18
Ceres, *1:* 201; *2:* 158, 169
Cethegus, *2:* 132
Chair of Peter, *1:* 243
Chaldean, *2:* 26
Chamillard, *1:* 4 n., 26 n.
Chanaanite, *2:* 58
Charon, *2:* 60, 128
Charybdis, *2:* 169
Chelidonius, *1:* xx, xxi, 95, 139 n., 180 n., 259
Cherubim, *1:* 24
chrism, *1:* 38, 44, 142, 262; *2:* 21, 92, 134, 193
Christ, *1:* 3, 5, 6, 8, 11, 15, 17, 22, 23, 24, 26, 28, 29, 31, 34, 35, 38, 39, 42, 43, 45, 52, 54, 56, 59, 63, 64, 72, 75, 78, 79, 83, 89, 90, 91, 92, 95, 97, 98, 99, 100, 101, 105, 110, 111, 117, 120, 121, 122, 123, 124, 125, 126, 128, 130, 131, 132, 134, 138,

139, 140, 143, 144, 146, 148, 149, 150, 151, 156, 157, 159, 164, 167, 168, 169, 170, 171, 172, 173, 175, 177, 179, 180, 182, 186, 188, 190, 192, 195, 198, 206, 209, 211, 213, 214, 215, 216, 217, 218, 219, 221, 225, 226, 230, 231, 238, 240, 242, 244, 245, 247, 249, 259, 262, 263, 266, 267, 268, 269, 270, 271, 272, 273, 275, 276, 277, 278; 2: 3, 5, 6, 9, 10, 13, 15, 16, 17, 18, 19, 20, 21, 22, 23, 24, 25, 27, 28, 29, 30, 32, 34, 35, 36, 37, 38, 39, 40, 43, 46, 55, 64, 69, 74, 81, 83, 84, 90, 93, 97, 98, 100, 101, 104, 105, 106, 107, 109, 110, 113, 114, 125, 131, 132, 133, 134, 139, 140, 141, 154, 156, 160, 162, 163, 164, 165, 172, 181, 185, 187, 188, 189, 190, 191, 192, 193, 194; Christ Crucified, *1:* 14, 171; *2:* 18, 192; Jesus Christ, *1:* 7, 54, 148, 178; as Judge, *1:* 50, 51, 68; as King, *1:* 12, 24, 29, 68, 81, 82, 85, 88, 92, 97, 101, 204, 213; *2:* 13, 81, 187; as Lamb, *1:* 22, 42; *2:* 195; as Mediator, *1:* 78; Messias, *1:* 191; Name of Christ, *1:* 43, 45, 121, 134, 196; *2:* 18; as Redeemer, *1:* 61, 77, 270; as Savior, *1:* 6, 14, 36, 54, 98, 140, 181, 272; *2:* 189, 192; as Shepherd, *1:* 57, 58, 263 n.; as Son of God, *1:* 38, 47, 87, 144, 148, 170, 192, 204, 216; *2:* 3, 6, 7, 10, 11, 13, 14, 15, 16, 19, 31, 34, 38, 39, 46, 56, 65; as Son of Man, *2:* 36, 107
Christian, *1:* 44, 55, 66, 72, 99 n., 108, 109, 122, 123, 131, 132, 148, 149, 160, 184, 193, 208, 209, 233, 244, 269, 271; *2:* 20, 21, 82, 84, 115, 131, 172
Church, *1:* 92, 107, 112, 117, 192, 243
Christmas Day, *1:* 78
Cicero, *1:* 41 n., 184 n., 197 n.; *2:* 117 n., 123 n., 132, 136
Claudia, *1:* 126
Claudian, *1:* 33 n., 36 n., 40 n., 98 n., 143 n., 183 n., 189 n., 243 n., 244 n., 249 n., 256 n., 257 n., 258 n., 259 n., 264 n., 271 n.; *2:* 5 n., 9 n., 48 n., 49 n., 50 n., 52 n., 53 n., 55 n., 89 n., 99 n., 104 n., 105 n., 116 n., 127 n., 128 n., 133 n., 142 n., 147 n., 154 n., 157 n., 158 n., 160 n., 162 n., 163 n., 164 n., 165 n., 170 n., 181 n.
Clement of Alexandria, *1:* 82 n., 85 n.
Cleopatra, *2:* 152
Cloacina, *2:* 12
Coan, *1:* 53
Cocytus, *2:* 119
Colline, *2:* 162
Columella, *2:* 104 n.
Compline, *1:* 39 n.
Complutum, *1:* 138 n.
Constantia, *1:* 274 n.
Constantine, *1:* 12 n., 25 n., 81 n., 126 n., 262 n., 264 n., 274 n.; *2:* 130, 131 n., 134 n.
Cordova, *1:* 138

INDEX 207

Corinth, 2: 152
Cornelius (Pope), 1: 242 n.
Cornelius (Sulla), 1: 132
Corvinus, 2: 158
Corybantes, 2: 157
Cossus, 1: 106
Cottian, 1: 126
Crassus, 2: 159
Crementius, 1: 145
Cremera, 2: 158
·Crete, 1: 33; 2: 156
Cross, 1: 29, 35, 44, 66, 83, 91,
 215, 218, 261; 2: 8, 20, 21, 92,
 94, 130, 131, 183, 185
Crown (Martyr's), 1: 66, 127,
 154, 180, 193; 2: 74
Cucuphas, 1: 139
Cumae, 2: 20
Curius, 2: 158
Cyanean, 2: 125
Cybehe, 1: 199
Cybele, 1: 234 n.; 2: 122 n.,
 135 n.
Cybeleian, 2: 157
Cyllenian, 2: 19
Cynic, 2: 12
Cynthius, 2: 156
Cyprian, St., 1: 3 n., 55 n., 66 n.,
 106 n., 266, 269, 270; 2: 117 n.,
 118 n., 146 n., 149 n., 156 n.
Cypris, 1: 200
Cytherea, 2: 12, 121, 156

Dacian, 1: 148, 151, 162
Dahan, 2: 166
Damasus, Pope, 1: xiii, xxi, 96 n.,
 106 n., 123 n., 127 n., 146 n.,
 156 n., 160 n., 172 n., 178 n.,
 180 n., 181 n., 231 n., 241 n.,

242 n., 243 n., 250 n., 252 n.,
 253 n., 257 n., 262 n., 263 n.,
 265 n., 271 n., 274 n., 275 n.,
 278 n., 279 n.
Daniel, 1: 27, 28
Danube, 2: 159, 162
David, 1: 86, 88, 226; 2: 19, 37,
 38, 62, 69, 93, 185
Decius, 2: 162
Delphi, 1: 198; 2: 20, 156
Deucalion, 1: 208 n.; 2: 15
Diana, 1: 203; 2: 20
Didache, 1: 46 n.
Dio, 2: 124 n.
Diocletian, 1: 95 n., 101 n., 128
 n., 132 n., 138 n., 142 n., 146
 n., 153 n., 182 n., 190 n., 284 n.
Diomede, 2: 158
Dis, 2: 128
Dives, 1: 76 n.
Docetists, 2: 36 n.
Dodona, 2: 20
Drusus, 2: 158
Dryades, 2: 125

Easter, 1: 30 n., 37 n., 60 n.
Ebionites, 2: 23
Egypt, 1: 33, 34, 90, 92, 120, 202;
 2: 12 n., 17, 60, 157
Elias, 1: 47, 161
Elim, 2: 183
Emerita, 1: 129 n.
Emeterius, 1: xx, 95, 139 n.,
 180 n.
Emmanuel, 1: 54; 2: 25
Encratia, 1: 138 n., 142, 143
Ephesus, 2: 156
Ephraim, 1: 92
Epiphany, 1: 83

208   INDEX

Epona, 2: 12
Ermini, F., 1: xxvi, 250 n.
Erycinus, 2: 122
Etna, 2: 125
Etruria, 1: 256
Etruscan, 2: 157
Eucharist, Holy, 1: 12 n., 26, 35, 64, 254; 2: 17, 20, 81, 93, 191
Eugene II, Archbishop of Toledo, 1: 141 n.
Eugenius, 2: 129 n.
Eulalia, St., of Barcelona, 1: 129 n.
Eulalia, St., of Merida, 1: 128, 129 n., 130, 136, 137, 259
Eulogius, 1: 168, 175
Eumorphio, 1: 163
Europe, 2: 156
Euphrates, 2: 60
Eusebius Pamphili, 1: 12 n., 32 n., 37 n., 101 n., 190 n., 240 n., 261 n., 262 n.; 2: 130 n., 261 n.
Evangelist, 1: 42
Evander, 2: 133
Eve, 2: 68, 179
Evotius, 1: 144
exorcism, 1: 45, 103; 2: 19
Exsultet, 1: 18 n., 38 n.
Ezechias, 2: 186

Fabian, Pope, 1: 240 n.
Fabius, 2: 158, 164
Fabricius, 2: 158
Falernian, 1: 61; 2: 93, 120
fasting, 1: 45, 46, 47, 48 n., 49, 52, 54, 55, 56, 57, 58, 170
Felix, St., of Gerona, 1: 139
Felix, St., of Saragossa, 1: 144
Flora, 2: 124, 158

Fortuna, 2: 122
Forum Cornelii, 1: 182
free will, 2: 66, 67, 69, 70, 155
Fronto, 1: 144
Fructuosus, St., 1: 138, 168, 169, 175

Gabine (cincture), 1: 234
Gabriel, 1: 123; 2: 187
Gades, 2: 123
Gaetulian, 2: 166
Gaiffier, B. de, 1: 146 n.
Gaius, 1: 145
Galaudian, 2: 166
Galerius, 1: 176, 192
Galileans, 2: 189
Gallienus, 1: 170, 268
Ganges, 2: 160
Ganymede, 1: 201; 2: 118, 124
Gauls, 1: 173; 2: 163
Gehenna, 1: 43, 83, 104; 2: 75, 96
Gelonians, 2: 19
Genesis, 2: 16
Genesius, St., 1: 139
genius (spirit), 2: 130, 143, 152, 153, 155
Gerasenes, 2: 19, 190
Gergesites, 2: 58
Germans, 2: 166
Gerona, 1: 139
Getae, 2: 19, 162
gladiators, 2: 128, 175, 176
Gnosius, 1: 217
God, 1: xxix, xxxi, 5, 9, 13, 14, 16, 20, 21, 23, 25, 26, 27, 32, 34, 37, 39, 40, 47, 48, 50, 53, 54, 57, 65, 67, 70, 73, 76, 78, 79, 82, 83, 84, 87, 89, 90, 92, 96, 97, 98, 100, 103, 105, 107,

108, 110, 111, 112, 116, 119, 120, 123, 124, 125, 127, 130, 137, 138, 140, 145, 147, 148, 151, 152, 153, 159, 164, 166, 169, 172, 173, 174, 180, 181, 189, 191, 204, 205, 206, 207, 208, 213, 214, 216, 219, 221, 223, 226, 243, 254, 256, 267, 268, 269, 270, 272; *2:* 3, 5, 6, 7, 8, 9, 11, 12, 13, 14, 15, 16, 17, 18, 20, 24, 25, 26, 27, 30, 31, 32, 33, 34, 36, 37, 38, 39, 43, 44, 45, 47, 48, 49, 50, 51, 53, 54, 55, 56, 57, 60, 62, 65, 66, 67, 69, 74, 79, 80, 81, 84, 91, 93, 97, 98, 100, 103, 105, 106, 107, 109, 110, 113, 116, 125, 126, 129, 131, 136, 142, 144, 145, 146, 148, 149, 151, 154, 156, 159, 160, 161, 164, 165, 166, 167, 168, 169, 173, 176, 179, 181, 182, 184, 186, 187, 192, 199, 200; the Almighty, *2:* 4, 10, 116, 160; as Creator, *1:* 23, 39, 67, 80, 131, 170, 231; *2:* 34, 45, 46, 48, 52, 54, 56, 126, 147; as Father, *1:* 14, 15, 18, 19, 21, 24, 26, 29, 35, 38, 39, 43, 45, 57, 60, 68, 69, 73, 75, 78, 79, 86, 87, 121, 129, 144, 148, 160, 176, 196, 198, 204, 205, 206, 213, 215, 216, 219, 222, 231, 264, 267, 270, 277, 278, 280; *2:* 3, 5, 6, 7, 8, 9, 11, 13, 14, 15, 16, 17, 23, 24, 27, 31, 32, 34, 36, 37, 38, 46, 47, 56, 65, 74, 81, 144, 159, 173, 187, 193, 199; as Maker, *1:* 46, 75, 121, 224; *2:* 27, 29, 31, 57;

Omnipotent, *2:* 102; Providence, *1:* 16; of Sabaoth, *1:* 25
Goliath, *2:* 69, 90, 185
Gomorrha, *1:* 153; *2:* 71, 79
Gorgon, *1:* 203
Gothic, *2:* 163
Gracchi, *2:* 133
Gradivus, *2:* 121
Greece, *1:* 92, 202; *2:* 18, 119, 171, 185
Gregory of Nazianzen, *1:* 66 n.; *2:* 266 n., 268 n.
Gregory of Nyssa, *1:* 81 n.
Guillen, J., *1:* xxvi

Habacuc, *1:* 27
Hades, *1:* 23
Hadrian, *1:* 265; *2:* 124
Hannibal, *2:* 162, 164
Hebrews, *1:* 34, 90, 120; *2:* 18, 69, 186
Hebrus, *2:* 19, 156
Hecate, *2:* 20
Hector, *2:* 152
Heider, A. B., *1:* 22 n.
Helena, St., *1:* 81 n.
Hellespont, *2:* 119
Hercules, *1:* 200, 201, 203, 228; *2:* 20, 57, 119
heresy, *2:* 5, 23, 36, 44, 47, 103, 105, 106, 185
Hermas, *1:* 46 n.
Herod, *1:* 88, 89; *2:* 188
Herrera, Isidoro Rodriguez, *1:* xv, xxvi, 220 n.
Hesperia, *2:* 160
Hethite, *2:* 58
Hevite, *2:* 58
Hiberia, *1:* 174

Hilary, St., of Poitiers, *1:* 60 n., 61 n., 62 n., 63 n., 64 n., 65 n., 66 n., 67 n.; *2:* 14 n., 15 n.
Hippocrates, *1:* 212
Hippolytus, St., *1:* 240, 242, 247, 252 n., 254, 257 n., 259
Hippolytus, Son of Theseus, *1:* 247 n.; *2:* 143
Holofernes, *2:* 83
Holy Saturday, *1:* 30 n., 31 n., 38 n.
Holy Spirit, *1:* 21, 25, 26 n., 38, 39, 59, 61, 75, 87, 172, 181, 195, 209, 219, 267, 271; *2:* 3, 5 n., 20, 24, 27, 28, 34, 50, 81, 105, 149, 165, 187, 188
Homer, *2:* 142
Honorius, *1:* 264; *2:* 141, 143, 161, 163, 164, 176
Honorius, Pope, *1:* 275 n.
Horace, *1:* xxix n., xxx n., 9 n., 10 n., 18 n., 30 n., 35 n., 48 n., 51 n., 55 n., 57 n., 58 n., 60 n., 62 n., 63 n., 71 n., 72 n., 74 n., 77 n., 97 n., 99 n., 109 n., 115 n., 121 n., 135 n., 138 n., 146 n., 148 n., 153 n., 170 n., 183 n., 195 n., 202 n., 212 n., 218 n., 238 n., 244 n., 275 n., 276 n., 279 n.; *2:* 18 n., 19 n., 52 n., 58 n., 146 n., 153 n., 159 n., 163 n., 172 n., 180 n.
Hun, *2:* 166
Hydra, *1:* 228
Hylas, *2:* 119
hymns, *1:* 3, 8, 14, 24, 29, 39, 45, 56, 59, 68, 69, 78, 83, 95, 101, 105, 128, 137, 168, 175, 176, 226, 273; *2:* 102

Hyrcanian, *2:* 19

Ida, *2:* 157
Idaean Mother, *1:* 197
Idalian, *2:* 154
idols, *1:* 101, 106, 124, 131, 134, 147, 148, 170, 209, 273, 275; *2:* 57, 93, 115, 129, 135, 142, 143, 154
Ignatius of Antioch, *1:* 84 n.
Ilian, *2:* 135
Illyrian, *1:* 176
Immaculate Conception, *1:* 21 n.
Incarnation, *1:* 21, 61, 80, 84, 87, 216; *2:* 24, 25, 26, 28, 30, 84, 93, 149, 187
India, *2:* 120
Indian, *1:* 203; *2:* 60, 170
Innocents, Holy, *1:* 89, 222; *2:* 188
Invocation of the Saints, *1:* 96, 97, 103, 104, 105, 127, 128, 137, 145, 166, 167, 172, 174, 175, 182, 183, 188, 189, 226, 239, 254, 255, 256, 257, 259, 265, 273, 280
Irenaeus, *1:* 87 n.
Isaac, *1:* 222
Isaia, *1:* 166; *2:* 25
Iscariot, *2:* 97, 199
Isidore of Seville, *1:* 3 n.
Isis, *1:* 132; *2:* 135, 156, 168
Israelites, *1:* 32, 33, 88, 90, 91, 99, 119, 131; *2:* 59, 101
Italus, *2:* 123
Italy, *1:* 273; *2:* 117, 119, 121, 149, 162

Jacob, *1:* 12, 92; *2:* 6, 59

INDEX 211

Janiculum, *1:* 244; *2:* 170
Janus, *1:* 123; *2:* 123
Jebusites, *2:* 58
Jeremia, *2:* 59
Jericho, *2:* 60, 88, 184
Jerome, St., *1:* xxix n., 3 n., 4 n., 5 n., 11 n., 22 n., 24 n., 27 n., 30 n., 44 n., 46 n., 57 n., 81 n., 82 n., 95 n., 101 n., 128 n., 166 n., 176 n., 182 n., 191 n., 240 n., 253 n., 256 n., 260 n., 264 n.; *2:* 133, 192
Jerusalem, *2:* 23 n., 107
Jesse, *1:* 86; *2:* 185
Jesus, *1:* 7, 54, 148, 178; *2:* 13, 19, 22, 35, 37, 39, 105, 187, 190
Jews, *1:* 82, 85; *2:* 16, 23, 59
Job, *2:* 86
John, the Baptist, *1:* 47, 48, 49, 160; *2:* 188, 190
John Chrysostom, St., *1:* 84 n., 85 n., 87 n., 190 n., 230 n.,
John, the Evangelist, *1:* 42, 43, 44, 191; *2:* 6, 8, 73, 195
Jonas, *1:* 50, 51, 52
Jonathan, *2:* 93
Jordan, *1:* 11, 91, 179; *2:* 60, 84, 183
Joseph, patriarch, *1:* 41, 42; *2:* 181
Josephus, *2:* 68 n.
Josue, *1:* 91
Jove, *1:* 106, 199, 201, 208, 272; *2:* 116, 118, 124, 125, 128, 134, 135, 162, 163, 167
Juda, *2:* 38, 93, 98
Judaea, *1:* 83, 85, 92, 119; *2:* 18, 19, 22
Judas (Iscariot), *2:* 191

Judgment, Last, *1:* 68, 82, 83, 138, 144, 175, 213, 239; *2:* 73, 74, 75, 147
Judith, *2:* 83
Jugurtha, *2:* 132
Julia, St., *1:* 144
Julian, the Apostate, *2:* 20, 22, 182 n.
Julian Code, *1:* 199
Julius, *2:* 159
Julus, *1:* 123
Juno, *1:* 200, 203; *2:* 12, 20, 118, 122, 124, 125, 156, 168
Jupiter, *1:* 170, 199, 202, 203, 208, 217; *2:* 118, 156, 161, 162, 164, 165
Justin, St., *1:* 81 n., 230 n., 274 n.
Justina, St., *1:* 266 n.
Justus, St., *1:* 130
Juvenal, *1:* xxix n., xxx n., 25 n., 52 n., 125 n., 196 n., 197 n., 202 n., 203 n., 215 n., 219 n., 256 n., 277 n.; *2:* 12 n., 49 n., 50 n., 54 n., 87 n., 98 n., 104 n., 134 n., 146 n., 150 n., 151 n., 158 n., 168 n.
Juvencus, *1:* 47 n., 54 n., 61 n., 85 n., 86 n., 87 n., 187 n.

Labarum, *2:* 130, 131
Lacedaemon, *2:* 157
Lachesis, *2:* 155
Laconian, *2:* 118
Lactantius, *1:* 37 n., 200 n., 236 n., 267 n.; *2:* 21 n., 54 n., 145 n., 146 n., 148 n., 149 n.
Lanciani, *1:* 126 n.
Lateran, *2:* 134
Latiaris, *2:* 128

Latin, *2:* 117, 128
Latona, *2:* 127
Lauds, *1:* 8 n., 146 n., 168 n., 274 n.
Laurentina, *2:* 158
Lavarenne, M., *1:* xix n., xxvi, 10 n., 54 n., 81 n., 91 n.; *2:* 189 n.
Laverna, *2:* 168
Lawrence, St., *1:* xx, xxi, 105, 106, 107, 108, 110, 111, 112, 113, 120, 121, 124, 127, 240 n., 241 n. 252 n., 257 n.
Lazarus, *1:* 63; *2:* 29, 30, 191
Lazarus (Eleazar in the parable of the Rich Man), *1:* 76
Leda, *2:* 118, 123
Lemnius, *1:* 200
Lent, *1:* 46 n.
Leo the Great, *1:* 66 n., 84 n., 87 n.
Leontinian, *2:* 170
Lerna, *1:* 228
Lethean, *1:* 40
Levi, *2:* 38, 97
Liber Pontificalis, *1:* 105 n., 107 n., 126 n., 241 n., 257 n., 262 n., 264 n., 275 n.
Liber (Bacchus), *1:* 202; *2:* 120
Libya, *1:* 266, 273; *2:* 20, 122, 156, 170
Liguria, *2:* 162
Lilybaeum, *2:* 170
Livia, *2:* 124, 125
Livy, *1:* 208
Lord, *1:* 12, 15, 22, 28, 29, 38, 49, 52, 55, 56, 69, 85, 92, 134, 170, 178, 179, 254, 261; *2:* 7, 12, 16, 17, 18, 19, 24, 25, 27, 28, 30, 32, 33, 34, 38, 39, 47, 49, 59, 64, 65, 93, 105, 113, 139, 140, 147, 167, 169, 180, 190, 192, 194
Lot, *2:* 67, 68, 69, 79, 80
Lot's wife, *2:* 68, 69
Lucan, *1:* xxix n., 73 n., 89 n., 163 n., 191 n., 197 n., 277 n., 278 n.; *2:* 101 n., 159 n., 166 n.
Lucifer (Morning Star), *1:* 36, 85; *2:* 26, 187
Lucina, *2:* 148
Lucretius, *1:* 9 n., 44 n., 59 n., 223 n.; *2:* 84 n.
Luke, *2:* 37
Luna, *2:* 127
Lupercalia, *1:* 197; *2:* 168
Luperci, *1:* 125
Lupercus, Martyr, *1:* 143
Lusitania, *1:* 129 n., 139
Lydia, *1:* 201 n.

Maccabees, *1:* 166, 222, 223
Macedonian, *2:* 158
Magi, *1:* 81 n., 84 n., 85, 86, 92; *2:* 25, 26
Mahony, Albertus, *1:* xxvi, 80 n., 170 n.
Maia, *2:* 118
Malmsbury, Willliam of, *1:* 257 n.
Mambre, *2:* 180
Mammon, *1:* 100; *2:* 58
Manasses, *1:* 92
Manichaean, *2:* 36, 37
Marchesi, C., *1:* xxvi, 106 n., 176 n.
Marcion, *2:* 44, 45, 46, 48, 49, 61
Marius, *2:* 132
Mars, *1:* 100, 208, 217; *2:* 121, 122, 125, 135, 156, 162

INDEX

Marsians, 2: 157
Martial (Roman poet), 1: 36 n.
Martial, St., 1: 144
Martinian, 1: 180 n.
martyrs, 1: 89, 95, 96, 97, 101, 103, 105, 107, 112, 119, 125, 128, 135, 137, 138, 140, 141, 142, 143, 144, 145, 146, 147, 148, 150, 151, 154, 157, 158, 159, 161, 165, 166, 168, 170, 172, 173, 176, 178, 180, 181, 182, 189, 190, 195, 207, 214, 218, 225, 229, 232, 238, 239, 240, 241, 242, 249, 250, 254, 255, 266, 272, 273, 279; 2: 82, 105, 161, 193, 194
martyrdom, 1: 89, 95 n., 96, 101, 105, 118, 127, 128 n., 138 n., 145 n., 146 n., 167, 168 n., 176 n., 182 n., 190 n., 222, 237, 260 n., 266 n., 272 n., 274 n.
Marucchi, 1: 252 n.
Matins, 1: 3 n., 95 n., 168 n.
Matthew, the Evangelist, 1: 191; 2: 37
Matuta, 2: 158
Maxentius, 2: 130
Maximian, 1: 132, 146 n.
Maximus, 2: 129 n.
Megaera, 2: 127
Megalesian, 2: 168
Melchisedech, 2: 80
Memphis, 2: 59, 157, 170
Mentor, 1: 203
Mercury, 1: 199; 2: 118, 157
Merida, 1: 128, 129 n., 136
Messenger, R. E., 1: 105 n.
Messias, 1: 191
Meyer, G., 1: 12 n., 18 n., 34 n.,

49 n., 67 n., 86 n., 129 n.
Minerva, 1: 203, 276; 2: 20, 157
Minucius Felix, 1: 15 n., 75 n., 76 n., 79 n., 108 n., 118 n., 149 n.; 2: 117 n., 122 n., 123 n., 128 n., 136 n., 147 n., 156 n.
Mithras, 2: 22 n.
Mithridates, 2: 158
Moab, 2: 69
Moses, 1: 32, 33, 34, 47, 90, 91; 2: 6, 7, 15, 16, 55, 181, 182, 183
Mount of Olives, 2: 193
Mozarabic Breviary, 1: 30 n., 39 n., 46 n., 60 n., 77 n., 95 n., 106 n., 129 n., 138 n., 146 n., 168 n., 241 n., 274 n.
Mozarabic Missal, 1: 30 n., 95 n., 146 n.
Mulvian Bridge, 2: 131
Myron, 1: 202

Narbonne, 1: 139
Nativity, 1: 21, 61, 78, 81, 82, 84, 86, 87, 89; 2: 25, 26, 83, 187
Naxos, 2: 122
Nazarene, 1: 45, 147, 192; 2: 133
Nebroth, 2: 49
Nemea, 2: 119
Neptune, 2: 125
Nero, 1: 95 n., 123, 260 n., 261; 2: 161
Neros (stepsons of Augustus), 2: 125
Nerva, 2: 125
Nestor, 1: 208
Nicene Council, 2: 81 n.
Nicene Creed, 1: 25 n.
Niceta of Remesiana, 1: 4 n.
Nile, 1: 33; 2: 102, 160, 168, 169

Ninive, *1:* 49, 51
Noe, *2:* 179
Noemi, *2:* 69
Nola, *1:* 256
None, *1:* 46 n.
Novatus, *1:* 242, 243
Numa, *1:* 122, 125, 208; *2:* 12, 119, 122, 142, 158
Numitor, *2:* 122
Nysa, *2:* 135

Olybrius, *2:* 133
Olympus, *2:* 118
Omphale, *1:* 201 n.
Optatus, *1:* 143
Orcus, *2:* 128
Origen, *1:* 81 n., 84 n.
Orpha, *2:* 69
Osiris, *2:* 136
Ostian Way, *1:* 261 n., 263
Ovid, *1:* 34 n., 44 n., 76 n., 197 n., 198 n., 200 n., 201 n., 204 n., 208 n.; *2:* 12 n., 57 n., 87 n., 103 n., 109 n., 113 n., 114 n., 116 n., 119 n., 120 n., 121 n., 128 n., 135 n., 149 n., 158 n., 167 n.

Palatine, *2:* 121
Palladium, *1:* 125; *2:* 122, 171
Palladius, *1:* 44 n.
Pallas, *2:* 122, 148, 156, 158, 169, 171
Pan, *1:* 201
Pannonia, *2:* 163
Paphian, *2:* 125, 159
Paraclete, *1:* 38, 209
Paradise, *1:* 36, 77; *2:* 71, 74
Parian, *1:* 255, 264; *2:* 148

Parthian, *2:* 13, 60, 61
Passion of Christ, *1:* 35, 36, 42, 45, 56, 58, 66, 67, 68, 77, 83, 91, 157, 171, 215, 216, 218, 261; *2:* 5, 8, 13, 17, 18, 23, 36, 39, 43, 65, 192, 195
Pastor, St., *1:* 139
Paul, Apostle, *1:* 123, 125, 243, 260, 261, 262, 263, 267; *2:* 61, 113, 114, 161, 194
Paul, of Narbonne, *1:* 139
Paulinus of Nola, *1:* xxix n., xxxi, 32 n., 37 n., 104 n., 125 n., 126 n., 145 n., 156 n., 239 n.; *2:* 81 n., 116 n., 133 n.
Pelusian, *2:* 170
Persephone, *2:* 21
Perses, *2:* 158
Persia, *1:* 85, 92, 206, *2:* 22 n., 59, 159
Peter, Apostle, *1:* 6, 123, 125, 178, 243, 260, 261, 262; *2:* 134, 139, 140, 161, 190, 194
Pharao, *1:* 33, 34, 42, 90; *2:* 17, 59, 181, 182
Pharos, *1:* 84; *2:* 17, 169
Pherezites, *2:* 58
Phidias, *1:* 203
Philip, Apostle, *2:* 9
Philip II of Macedon, *1:* 110
Philistines, *2:* 60, 185
Phlegethon, *1:* 23; *2:* 71, 128
Phoebus, *2:* 135
Photinus, *2:* 106
Phrygia, *1:* 122; *2:* 121, 122, 156, 171
Picinum, *1:* 256
Picus, *2:* 123
Pilate, *2:* 18

Pinarian, 2: 119
Planella, J., 1: xxvi
Plato, 2: 12, 117
Plautus, 1: 200 n.
Pliny the Elder, 2: 54, 63
Pluto, 1: 150; 2: 127, 128
Po, 2: 162
Pohle-Preuss, 1: 25, 49
Pollentia, 2: 163
Pollux, 2: 20, 123
Polyclites, 1: 202
Pomerium, 1: 252
Pompey, 2: 23
Pompilius, 1: 208
Pontian, Pope, 1: 240 n.
Pontius, 1: 267 n.
Pope, R. Martin, 1: xxvi, 24 n.
Priam, 2: 171
Priapus, 1: 201; 2: 119, 168
Primitivus, St., 1: 144
Probi, 2: 133
Propertius, 2: 12
Proserpine, 1: 201; 2: 21, 127
Prudentius, 1: 128
Pseudo-Athanasius, 1: 19, 46 n., 56 n.
Pseudo-Matthew, 1: 81 n.
Publius, St., 1: 144
Punic, 1: 140, 266; 2: 148, 164, 170
Purgatory, 1: 172; 2: 75
Pyrenees, 1: 126, 174
Pyrrha, 1: 208
Pyrrhus, 2: 158

Quintilianus, St., 1: 144
Quirinus (Martyr), 1: 176, 178
Quirinus (Romulus), 1: 121; 2: 133, 150

Rahab, 2: 184
Red Sea, 1: 33, 34, 164; 2: 60, 101, 102, 182
relics, 1: 136, 137, 138, 139, 141, 143, 159, 167, 174, 251
Remus, 1: 122; 2: 150, 153
Resurrection, 1: 6, 23, 24, 36, 71, 72, 76, 87, 145; 2: 39, 40, 65, 147, 167, 193
Rhea Silvia, 2: 121
Rhine, 2: 159
Rhodians, 2: 156
Rhodopeian, 2: 19
Rogatianus, 1: 169 n.
Romanus, St., 1: 190, 193, 194, 215, 224, 227, 230, 234, 239
Rome, 1: xxxi, 105, 107, 117, 121, 122, 123, 124, 125, 126, 127, 140, 147, 150, 182, 189, 192, 198, 202, 208, 241, 244, 247, 256, 258, 260, 264, 265, 268, 274; 2: 18, 20, 116, 121, 123, 124, 125, 127, 131, 132, 133, 134, 136, 141, 143, 150, 151, 152, 154, 155, 156, 157, 158, 159, 160, 161, 165, 166, 170, 175, 176
Romulus, 1: 122, 208, 216, 240, 264, 274; 2: 115, 116, 153
Ruth, 2: 69

Saba, 1: 72, 87
Sabaoth, 1: 25
Sabaria, 1: 176 n.
Sabbath, 2: 22, 37
Sabellius, 2: 5, 11
Sabine, 2: 119
Sabinus, 2: 123
Sacred Way, 2: 123

Sacrifice of the Mass, *1:* 30 n., 37, 55, 165, 258, 265
Saguntum, *1:* 142
Salarian Way, *2:* 128
Salia, *1:* xxx
Samnites, *1:* 256
Samson, *2:* 184
Samuel, *2:* 93
Sara, *2:* 80, 180
Saragossa, *1:* 137, 140, 141 n., 143, 145
Sardinian, *2:* 170
Sarmatian, *2:* 166
Satan, *1:* 20, 21, 28, 45, 50, 54, 55, 67, 77, 79, 98, 125, 140, 142, 192, 279; *2:* 5, 19, 49, 50, 51, 57, 58, 59, 60, 61, 62, 64, 65, 67, 103, 179
Saturn, *1:* 123, 199; *2:* 12, 117, 123, 135, 150
Saturnalia, *2:* 167
Saturnia (Juno), *2:* 124
Saturnia (town), *2:* 117
Saturninus, *1:* 144
Saul (St. Paul), *2:* 194
Saxon, *2:* 166
Scantinian Law, *1:* 199
Schuster, I., *1:* 30, 180
Scot, *2:* 12
Scripture, Holy, *1:* 49, 61, 101 n., 153, 217, 243, 267; *2:* 13, 15, 16, 19, 25, 37, 38, 48, 50, 54, 56, 64, 67, 69, 80
Scythia, *1:* 92; *2:* 19, 150
Senate, *1:* 123, 150; *2:* 123, 124, 131, 133, 134, 135, 143, 154
Seneca, *1:* 37 n., 38 n., 50 n., 65 n., 66 n., 96 n., 138 n., 147 n., 155 n., 220 n., 228 n., 247 n., 268 n., 278 n.; *2:* 72 n.. 155 n., 186 n.
Senones, *2:* 162
Seraphim, *1:* 24
Serapis, *2:* 157, 168
Serra-Vilaro, J., *1:* 168 n.
Severus, *2:* 125
Sext, *1:* 46 n.
Sibyl, *2:* 169
Sibylline books, *2:* 20
Sicily, *2:* 150, 170
Sign of the Cross, *1:* 44, 45, 66; *2:* 21, 22, 92, 134
Siloe, Pool of, *2:* 28, 189
S. Silviae peregrinatio, *1:* 3 n., 4 n., 8 n., 30 n., 37 n.
Simeon, *2:* 38
Simon (Peter), *2:* 139
sin, *1:* 8, 20, 21, 23, 44, 49, 60, 77, 114, 115, 116, 167; *2:* 7, 8, 34, 35, 50, 51, 52, 53, 57, 61, 62, 66, 67, 70, 93, 155, 171
Sion, *2:* 59
Sirius, *1:* 84
Siscia, *1:* 176
Sixt, G., *1:* 247 n.
Sixtus II, Pope, *1:* 105 n., 106, 107
Smith, E. G., *1:* xxvi
Socrates, historian, *1:* 121 n.
Sodom, *1:* 153; *2:* 16, 67, 68, 69, 79, 82
Solomon, *2:* 22, 63, 106, 185, 194
soul *1:* 16, 19, 23, 40, 41, 69, 70, 71, 206; *2:* 31, 32, 33, 34, 35, 44, 45, 47, 61, 62, 64, 70, 71, 72, 73, 74, 79, 81, 82, 84, 104, 105, 109, 110, 147, 152, 160, 172, 179

Souter, A., *1:* 22 n.
Sozamen, *1:* 121 n.
Spain, *1:* 96, 126, 168, 174, 273; *2:* 160
Stam, J., *1:* xxvi
Statius, *2:* 83 n., 109 n., 110 n., 115 n., 133 n., 167 n.
Stephen, St., *1:* 120; *2:* 193
Sterculus, *1:* 123
Stilicho, *2:* 163, 164
Styx, *1:* 36; *2:* 13, 49, 97, 127
Subura, *1:* 244
Successus, St., *1:* 144
Suetonius, *2:* 124
Sulla, *1:* 182
Sulpicius Severus, *1:* 82 n., 100 n., 104 n.
Symmachus, *2:* 115, 135, 140, 141, 143, 144 n., 149, 151, 152, 153 n., 156 n., 157, 159, 161, 164, 165, 169
Symmachus, Pope, *1:* 275 n.
Synna, *2:* 148
Syrtis, *1:* 80; *2:* 20, 152

Tacitus, *2:* 199
Tagus, *2:* 159
Tarentum, *2:* 164
Tarpeian, *1:* 150; *2:* 22, 133
Tarragona, *1:* 138, 168, 174, 175
Tartarus, *1:* 269; *2:* 71
Tauric rites, *2:* 128
Taurobolium, *1:* 234, 235
Terce, *1:* 46 n.
Terminus, *2:* 172
Tertullian, *1:* xviii, xix, 3 n., 11 n., 19 n., 23 n., 30 n., 35 n., 39 n., 40 n., 41 n., 42 n., 45 n., 46 n., 56 n., 60 n., 72 n., 75 n., 99 n., 103 n., 166 n., 171 n., 200 n., 203 n., 230 n., 255 n., 276 n.; *2:* 11 n., 13 n., 48 n., 56 n., 87 n., 117 n., 118 n., 146 n., 147 n., 150 n., 152 n., 156 n., 165 n., 175 n.
Thackeray, F. S., *1:* xxvi
Tharsis, *1:* 50
Thascius (Cyprian), *1:* 266 n., 272
Thebes, *2:* 120, 150
Theodosius I, *1:* 124, 264; *2:* 116, 117, 129, 132, 135, 141, 142, 161, 176
Theodota, *1:* 191 n.
Theodolus, *1:* 191 n.
Thessalian witchcraft, *1:* 227; *2:* 21, 118
Thomson, H. J., *1:* xxvi, 70 n.; *2:* 104
Thrace, *1:* 92
Thule, *2:* 72
Thunderer (God), *1:* 42, 87, 172; *2:* 11, 57, 66, 101
Thunderer (Jupiter), *1:* 200, 203
Tiber, *1:* 244, 254, 260, 262, 265; *2:* 131, 160, 168, 170
Tibullus, *1:* 125 n.; *2:* 91 n., 170 n.
Tiro, *1:* 184 n.
Tirynthius, *1:* 201
Titus, *2:* 23, 125
Tobias, *1:* 73
Toledo, Council of, *1:* 25 n.
Trajan, *1:* 95 n.; *2:* 125
Trinity, Blessed, *1:* 15, 21, 25, 38, 39, 75, 168; *2:* 3, 5 n., 11, 13, 47, 74, 81, 105

Triplolemus, 2: 169
Tritonia, 2: 159
Trivia, 2: 127, 143
Tros, 2: 123
Troy, 2: 122, 171
Tullius, 2: 136
Tullus, 2: 122
Tyre, 2: 60
Tyrrhenium, 1: 244

Ulysses, 2: 158
Urban, St., 1: 144
Urban, Pope, 1: 240 n.
Utica, 1: 272 n.

Valencia, 1: 142
Valerian (Bishop), 1: x, 240, 241 n., 250, 259
Valerian (emperor), 1: 105 n., 107, 109, 110, 117, 168 n., 182 n., 265 n., 266 n., 268
Valerius, 1: x, 141
Vandals, 2: 166
Vascons, 1: 103, 126
Vatican Hill, 1: 262, 265; 2: 134
Venetian, 2: 162
Venus, 1: 132, 200 n., 202; 2: 121, 122, 123, 124, 125, 135, 148, 157, 158
Vergil, 1: 3 n., 4 n., 5 n., 7 n., 9 n., 10 n., 13 n., 15 n., 16 n., 17 n., 18 n., 19 n., 20 n., 21 n., 22 n., 23 n., 24 n., 25 n., 27 n., 31 n., 33 n., 35 n., 36 n., 37 n., 39 n., 40 n., 45 n., 50 n., 51 n., 52 n., 53 n., 54 n., 55 n., 56 n., 57 n., 58 n., 59 n., 60 n., 62 n., 64 n., 65 n., 66 n., 67 n., 69 n., 71 n., 73 n., 74 n., 75 n., 76 n., 78 n., 79 n., 80 n., 86 n., 96 n., 97 n., 98 n., 100 n., 101 n., 102 n., 103 n., 104 n., 119 n., 121 n., 122 n., 123 n., 124 n., 126 n., 130 n., 131 n., 134 n., 135 n., 136 n., 137 n., 138 n., 140 n., 154 n., 155 n., 160 n., 161 n., 164 n., 165 n., 170 n., 171 n., 172 n., 173 n., 174 n., 176 n., 177 n., 179 n., 180 n., 181 n., 182 n., 183 n., 185 n., 187 n., 188 n., 194 n., 196 n., 197 n., 199 n., 201 n., 202 n., 208 n., 218 n., 220 n., 222 n., 224 n., 227 n., 231 n., 234 n., 243 n., 244 n., 245 n., 248 n., 251 n., 255 n., 258 n., 259 n., 263 n., 264 n., 265 n., 269 n., 270 n., 272 n., 273 n., 276 n., 278 n., 279 n.; 2: 7 n., 10 n., 12 n., 13 n., 16 n., 18 n., 19 n., 20 n., 21 n., 25 n., 27 n., 38 n., 45 n., 48 n., 49 n., 51 n., 52 n., 53 n., 54 n., 56 n., 58 n., 60 n., 61 n., 68 n., 69 n., 70 n., 72 n., 73 n., 81 n., 82 n., 83 n., 84 n., 85 n., 87 n., 88 n., 89 n., 90 n., 91 n., 92 n., 94 n., 95 n., 96 n., 97 n., 98 n., 99 n., 100 n., 101 n., 102 n., 103 n., 105 n., 106 n., 107 n., 108 n., 109 n., 110 n., 113 n., 115 n., 117 n., 118 n., 119 n., 120 n., 121 n., 122 n., 123 n., 125 n., 126 n., 127 n., 131 n., 132 n., 133 n., 141 n., 143 n., 146 n., 148 n., 150 n., 151 n., 156 n., 157 n., 158 n., 160 n., 162 n., 163 n., 164 n., 166 n., 168 n., 169 n.,

INDEX   219

170 n., 171 n., 172 n., 173 n.,   Vincent, St., *1:* xx, 141, 142, 146,
  174 n., 175 n., 180 n., 186 n.,   147, 156
  187 n., 190 n.   Virgin Mary, *1:* 14, 20, 21, 45,
Vespers, *1:* xvi, 30 n., 39 n., 60 n.,   48, 61, 78, 80, 82; *2:* 7, 8, 9,
  95 n., 129 n., 146 n., 191 n.,   11, 20, 23, 24, 25, 26, 28, 35, 38,
  274 n.   39, 63, 65, 83, 84, 93, 187, 188
Vesta, *1:* 125; *2:* 122, 169, 171,   Vives, J., *1:* xxi, 250 n., 257 n.
  174   Vulcan, *1:* 119, 121; *2:* 125, 135
Vestal Virgins, *1:* 126; *2:* 169,
  171, 172, 174, 175   Waszink, J. H., *1:* 19 n.
Vettonia, *1:* 136   Word, of God, *1:* 14, 21, 39, 45,
Via Nomentana, *1:* 274 n.   78, 79, 80, 205; *2:* 3, 7, 8, 9, 10,
Via Tiburtina, *1:* 106 n., 126 n.,   14, 19, 23, 84
  240 n., 252 n., 257 n.
Vigilius, Pope, *1:* 252 n.   Zoilus, *1:* 138
vigils, *1:* 30 n., 37 n., 105, 265   Zoroaster, *2:* 22

INDEX
OF HOLY SCRIPTURE

(Books of the Old Testament)

Genesis, *1*:12 n., 19 n., 20 n., 21 n., 41 n., 85 n., 153 n., 160 n., 196 n., 222 n., 226 n., 279 n.; *2*:6 n., 15 n., 16 n., 27 n., 31 n., 33 n., 38 n., 43 n., 49 n., 51 n., 52 n., 54 n., 55 n., 58 n., 66 n., 67 n., 68 n., 79 n., 80 n., 88 n., 179 n., 180 n., 181 n., 194 n.

Exodus, *1*:32 n., 33 n., 34 n., 35 n., 47 n., 50 n., 83 n., 90 n., 91 n., 119 n., 120 n., 131 n., 164 n., 172 n.; *2*:6 n., 7 n., 15 n., 16 n., 17 n., 59 n., 60 n., 93 n., 101 n., 102 n., 181 n., 182 n., 183 n.

Leviticus, *2*:37 n.

Numbers, *1*:35 n., 86 n.; *2*:60 n., 98 n., 109 n., 183 n.

Deuteronomy, *1*:28 n., 47 n., 50 n.; *2*:67 n.

Josue, *1*:91 n., 179 n.; *2*:58 n., 60 n., 98 n., 184 n.

Judges, *2*:184 n.

Ruth, *2*:69 n.

1 Kings, *2*:90 n., 93 n., 94 n., 185 n.

2 Kings, *1*:50 n.; *2*:62 n.

3 Kings, *1*:47 n., 161 n.; *2*:106 n., 107 n., 185 n.

4 Kings, *1*:47 n.; *2*:59 n., 186 n.

4 Esdras *1*:55 n.

Tobias, *1*:55 n., 73 n.

Judith, *2*:83 n.

Job, *1*:41 n., 68 n., 239 n., 261 n.; *2*:34 n., 86 n.

Psalms, *1*:11 n., 12 n., 15 n., 16 n., 18 n., 24 n., 25 n., 29 n., 50 n., 57 n., 60 n., 61 n., 68 n., 69 n., 78 n., 87 n., 92 n., 164 n., 179 n., 191 n., 205 n., 226 n.; *2*:5 n., 8 n., 23 n., 186 n.

Proverbs, *1*:79 n.; *2*:108 n., 126 n., 144 n.

Wisdom, *1*:15 n.; *2*:31 n., 32 n., 142 n.

Sirach (Ecclus.), *1*:78 n., 91 n., 147 n.; *2*:67 n., 144 n., 169 n.
Isaia, *1*:12 n., 22 n., 24 n., 31 n., 54 n., 81 n., 82 n., 86 n., 87 n., 213 n.; *2*:25 n., 50 n., 144 n., 145 n.
Jeremia, *1*:25 n., 67 n.
Ezechiel, *1*:50 n., 68 n., 270 n.
Daniel, *1*:24 n., 26 n., 69 n., 173 n.; *2*:10 n., 59 n.
Joel, *1*:11 n., 81 n.
Jona, *1*:49 n., 50 n., 51 n., 52 n., 53 n.
Michea, *1*:87 n.
Malachia, *1*:120 n.
2 Machabees, *1*:166 n., 222 n., 223 n., 224 n.

(BOOKS OF THE NEW TESTAMENT)

Matthew, *1*:6 n., 29 n., 47 n., 48 n., 54 n., 55 n., 56 n., 57 n., 61 n., 62 n., 63 n., 64 n., 65 n., 67 n., 82 n., 83 n., 85 n., 86 n., 87 n., 88 n., 100 n., 110 n., 123 n., 138 n., 150 n., 160 n., 178 n., 191 n., 216 n., 218 n., 222 n., 231 n., 239 n., 279 n.; 2:3 n., 5 n., 8 n., 11 n., 16 n., 25 n., 26 n., 27 n., 36 n., 37 n., 62 n., 69 n., 72 n., 74 n., 75 n., 90 n., 97 n., 99 n., 100 n., 101 n., 105 n., 106 n., 109 n., 139 n., 165 n., 169 n., 173 n., 174 n., 187 n., 188 n., 189 n., 190 n., 191 n., 192 n., 193 n.

Mark, *1*:3 n., 6 n., 23 n., 62 n., 63 n., 64 n., 65 n., 68 n., 164 n., 171 n.; 2:19 n., 23 n., 27 n., 28 n., 69 n., 71 n., 98 n., 100 n., 139 n., 190 n., 192 n.

Luke, *1*:6 n., 12 n., 23 n., 29 n., 48 n., 49 n., 57 n., 61 n., 62 n., 63 n., 65 n., 77 n., 87 n., 88 n., 95 n., 117 n., 238 n., 261 n.; 2:24 n., 25 n., 26 n., 37 n., 38 n., 72 n., 74 n., 83 n., 100 n., 149 n., 187 n., 188 n., 190 n., 192 n., 193 n.

John, *1*:6 n., 21 n., 26 n., 39 n., 43 n., 56 n., 57 n., 60 n., 61 n., 62 n., 63 n., 64 n., 65 n., 66 n., 68 n., 75 n., 79 n., 83 n., 114 n., 148 n., 181 n., 215 n., 221 n., 259 n.; 2:3 n., 6 n., 8 n., 9 n., 13 n., 18 n., 23 n., 24 n., 27 n., 28 n., 30 n., 31 n., 32 n., 34 n., 50 n., 56 n., 64 n., 74 n., 139 n., 147 n., 189 n., 191 n., 192 n., 193 n.

Acts of the Apostles, *1*:23 n., 25 n., 49 n., 59 n., 68 n., 107 n., 109 n., 120 n., 147 n.; 2:22 n., 23 n., 49 n., 98 n., 106 n., 113 n., 139 n., 191 n., 193 n., 194 n.

Romans, *1*:3 n., 25 n., 26 n., 83 n., 207 n.; 2:17 n., 31 n., 35 n., 36 n., 39 n., 57 n., 61 n., 199 n.

1 Corinthians, *1*:11 n., 15 n., 21 n., 23 n., 25 n., 28 n., 31 n., 67 n., 83 n., 91 n., 150 n., 191 n., 206 n., 215 n., 216 n.; 2:4 n., 11 n., 17 n., 32 n., 39 n., 40 n., 83 n., 105 n., 146 n., 147 n., 149 n.

2 Corinthians, *1*:100 n., 152 n., 206 n., 211 n., 239 n.; 2:16 n., 34 n., 35 n.

Galatians, *1*:218 n.; 2:57 n., 79 n., 110 n.

Ephesians, *1*:31 n., 206 n.; 2: 35 n., 46 n., 57 n., 60 n., 61 n., 62 n., 81 n., 106 n.

Philippians, *1*:43 n., 80 n., 121 n., 262 n., 271 n.; 2:46 n.

Colossians, *1*:79 n., 270 n.; 2: 8 n., 31 n., 50 n., 129 n.

1 Thessalonians, *1*:3 n., 83 n.
2 Thessalonians, *1*:43 n.
1 Timothy, *1*:78 n., 204 n., 270 n.; 2:8 n., 53 n.
2 Timothy, *1*:123 n., 242 n., 261 n., 262 n.; 2:199 n.
Hebrews, *1*:13 n., 43 n., 47 n., 87 n., 92 n., 121 n., 211 n., 267 n.; 2:8 n., 13 n., 22 n., 37 n., 46 n., 80 n., 81 n., 109 n.
James, *1*:25 n., 89 n., 97 n., 146 n., 2:90 n.
1 Peter, *1*:3 n., 28 n., 65 n., 89 n.; 2:4 n., 54 n., 62 n., 90 n.
2 Peter, *1*:83 n.; 2:34 n., 84 n.
Apocalypse of St. John the Apostle, *1*:42 n., 43 n., 82 n., 83 n., 92 n., 95 n., 117 n., 145 n., 146 n., 147 n., 174 n., 213 n., 239 n., 263 n.; 2:72 n., 73 n., 101 n., 107 n., 108 n., 195 n.

www.ingramcontent.com/pod-product-compliance
Lightning Source LLC
Chambersburg PA
CBHW032034290426
44110CB00012B/792